What others are

"This book is a must for people who would like to be vegetarian, but thought it was too complicated and time-consuming an endeavor. Mainstream food processors and retailers are now making hundreds of completely vegetarian food products that are delicious, nutritious, and easy to prepare. Davis has taken the next step by bringing these foods home to practicing vegans and transitioning vegetarians, alike."

- Alex Hershaft, Ph.D., President,
Farm Animal Reform Movement

"Finally, a guide that takes you by the hand to the best vegetarian food available on the market. It's a map, it's a menu, it's a must have for every wanna be and experienced vegetarian."

- Kevin Nealon
Actor/Comedian

". . . Makes vegetarian eating as easy as pie. A couch potato's dream guide to eating healthy snacks and meals. It made me so hungry I had to race to the grocery store."

- Ingrid E. Newkirk, President
People for the Ethical Treatment of Animals

"When we strip aside all the geegaws and gadgets that we spend far too much of our time in pursuit of, we are left with the one thing we truly need...a good meal. Gail Davis has provided easy access to one and all to make healthy and sustainable choices in their diet. Dig in, you're in for some of the tastiest food you've ever sampled."

- Ed Begley, Jr.
Actor/Environmentalist

"This book is a valuable resource for anyone looking for better health through convenience foods."

- John McDougall, M.D. and Mary McDougall
Authors of *The McDougall Program for a Healthy Heart*

"With this handy guide, excuses disappear. No longer can one say, 'I'd eat vegetarian but I can't cook,' or 'I don't know what to eat,' or 'It's too difficult.' *So, Now What do I Eat?* is a food reference bible that gives you the shortcuts. Davis proves that eating vegetarian can be fast, easy, and delicious!"

- Marr Nealon, President,
Voice for a Viable Future

"A vegetarian diet is now recognized by enlightened mainstream medical professionals as the means of preventing heart disease, various cancers, and many other illnesses. This superb book now makes it so much easier for anyone to choose healthy, plant-based meals." - Robert Baker, M.D., Director,
Low Fat Lifestyle Program

"At last, a book for people who want to eat well, but 'don't have time to cook.' Gail Davis has done a masterful job, sleuthing out ready-to-eat foods that are healthful and great tasting. I will be recommending it to all my students."

- Jennifer Raymond
Author of *The Peaceful Palate*

"Finally, the book that everyone has been waiting for! Now no one can say that eating healthy isn't convenient. *So, Now What Do I Eat?* is destined to become a staple in every health conscious home in America." - Linda Blair
Actress

"It's a question I'm asked a thousand times a year; now all I have say is read Gail Davis' book, *So, Now What Do I Eat?* It's terrific and I loved it!' - Howard F. Lyman, President
International Vegetarian Union

So, Now What Do I Eat?

So, Now What Do I Eat?

The Complete Guide to
Vegetarian Convenience Foods

Gail Davis

Foreword by Neal Barnard, M.D.

Corrales, New Mexico

So, Now What Do I Eat?
The Complete Guide To
Vegetarian Convenience Foods

By Gail Davis

Published by:
Blue Coyote Press
Post Office Box 2101
Corrales, New Mexico 87048-2101
U.S.A.

10 9 8 7 6 5 4 3 2 1
This book is manufactured in the United States of America.

Cover design by Foster & Foster, Inc.
Logo design by Chris Hahn

Publisher's Cataloging-in-Publication
  (Provided by Quality Books, Inc.)

Davis, Gail Barbara.
    So, now what do i eat : the complete guide to vegetarian convenience foods / Gail Davis ; foreword by Neal Barnard. -- 1st ed.
    p. cm.
    Includes indexes.
    Preassigned LCCN: 97-75324
    ISBN: 0-9660296-0-7
    1. Vegetarian cookery. 2. Convenience Foods.
3. Low-Cholesterol foods. I. Title.

TX837.D38 1998   QBI97-41163
641.5'636

In loving memory of my father Marty Davis, whose kind, gentle, spirit will forever dwell within my heart.

Acknowledgments

For all of your love, support, encouragement, kindness, and faith in me, I would like to extend my most heartfelt appreciation to my beautiful mother, Edie Davis, my darling cousin, Bonnie Weissberg, and my dearest friends and associates, Parandeh Tabarestani, Robert Baker, M.D., Marr Nealon, Howard Lyman, Patti Breitman, Jennifer Raymond and Stephen Avis, Alex Hershaft, Ph.D., Simon Oswitch, Pma Tregenza, Merrill Tilker, Justin and Barbara Kolb, Sandra Soule, Kannan Nadarajan, and Roger Jacobson.

For your unique ideas and contributions of time, energy, and talent, many special thanks to Linda Nealon, Kirk Kernen, Neal Barnard, M.D., Chris Hahn, George Foster, Chiu-Nan Lai, Steve Marquez, Wally Danalevich, Dan Poynter, Gary, Vina, Sean, and staff at Lassen Family Foods in Goleta, California, and Benjamin, Ken, Mark, and all of the outstanding librarians at the Santa Barbara Public Library.

I am eternally grateful to John Robbins for writing *Diet for a New America*, an empowering gift that transformed my life into one filled with greater awareness, compassion and purpose.

Finally, I owe a special debt of gratitude to Michael Panarese for coming back into my life and reigniting the flame of inspiration. The light of your love helped me to regain my focus. You are truly the brightest star in the sky.

Disclaimer

This book is designed to provide information in regard to the subject matter covered. It is sold with the understanding that the publisher and the author are not engaged in rendering nutritional counseling or medical advice. If such advice is warranted, the services of a competent professional should be sought.

Every effort has been made to make this book as complete and as accurate as possible. However, there may be mistakes both typographical and in content. Therefore, this text should be used only as a general guide. Furthermore, new products are always being introduced into the market while others may be discontinued. You are urged to explore the aisles of your local natural foods store and supermarket to learn what is available. ALWAYS read product labels.

For more information on vegetarianism and related subjects, contact the many organizations listed in the Appendix.

The purpose of this book is to inform and entertain. The author and Blue Coyote Press shall have neither liability nor responsibility to any person or entity with respect to loss or damage caused, or alleged to be caused, directly or indirectly by the information contained in this book.

If you do not wish to be bound by the above, you may return this book to the publisher for a full refund.

Contents

Foreword

We are all rethinking our diets. We aim to slim down, lower our cholesterol levels, reduce the risk of cancer and heart disease, or bring down our blood pressure. Some of us just want to live longer. Or it may be that the recognition of environmental or animal rights issues motivates us to dump out the drumsticks and ham. But, then comes the question: So, now what do I eat?

As we wander down unfamiliar aisles at the grocery store and read strange ingredients in recipe lists, we ask ourselves if we really have time for healthy eating. We are torn between the convenience of greasy fast foods and the daunting prospect of relearning how to cook and how to eat, wondering if we'll ever be on terra firma again.

It gets even more complicated when you enter a health food store. Twenty years ago, health food stores were dusty, cramped places, staffed by folks in tie-died shirts who knew all 12 products on their shelves.

No more. Health food stores are now huge supermarkets with shelves overflowing with foods we once only dreamt of: Hot dogs, Canadian bacon, and burgers that taste exactly like the real thing, but with no cholesterol or animal fat at all; and milk that comes from rice or soy, rather than from a cow, giving the consumer dozens of flavors ready to splash on cereal, with no animal proteins or lactose.

So, Now What Do I Eat? presents a banquet of choices for those who are looking for convenience without sacrificing taste. Gail Davis walks down the grocery aisle with you and shows you the best choices to suit your own needs. She knows

1

the challenges of changing your personal menu, having first revamped her own diet years ago and having worked ever since to help others repair theirs. She shares her intimate knowledge of how to make sense of healthy eating and how to avoid its pitfalls.

So, Now What Do I Eat? is a quick guide that should be on your kitchen counter next to your grocery list and in your glove compartment as you head to the store. It will save you hours of time shopping and will let you skip embarrassing purchases when you're shopping for others. It lets you make the change to healthier fare quickly and with confidence.

As you look over the wealth of practical material presented here, let me add four quick tips:

• Focus on exploration, not deprivation. For now, at least, you are experimenting, trying new tastes, new products, and maybe a new store or two. There will be many delights and probably an occasional dud. That's okay. It's what experimenting is all about.

• Transition foods can really help. Foods that look and taste like meat but that are actually vegetarian can lure even the most dyed-in-the-wool omnivore to a healthier diet.

• Be strict with yourself. Just as smokers have a harder time if they have an occasional cigarette, it is harder to leave fatty foods behind if every once in awhile you tease your taste buds with Kentucky Fried Chicken. A complete break is much easier.

• Focus on the short term. As you make a dietary change, only do it for three weeks. Throw out the animal products and added oils, and be strict about it, but do it only for three weeks. This kind of short-term test is much easier than the daunting prospect of a permanent change. After three weeks, you will likely find that you have lost weight, your blood pressure and cholesterol will probably have dropped, and your energy level will have improved noticeably. If you like the way you feel, you can stick with it.

The wisdom that Gail Davis has packed into these pages will make the transition to healthier eating a joy.

Neal D. Barnard, M.D.
President
Physicians Committee for Responsible Medicine

Introduction
Why Vegetarian?

. . . .

As long as man continues to be the ruthless destroyer of lower living beings, he will never know health or peace. For as long as men massacre animals, they will kill each other. Indeed, he who sows the seeds of murder and pain cannot reap joy and love.
-Pythagoras

On April 16, 1996, Howard Lyman, an ex-fourth generation cattle rancher and Director of The Humane Society's Eating with Conscience Campaign, made an unprecedented appearance on the Oprah Winfrey Show. While 20 million stunned viewers tuned in, Mr. Lyman described many of the horrible secrets of modern factory farming, including the beef industry's practice of feeding ground up cow remains to cattle. As in-studio cameras scanned the audience's shocked faces and microphones captured their gasps and groans, Americans learned yet another compelling reason to kick the meat habit. Sharing the stage with Mr. Lyman was Dr. Gary Weber, a National Cattleman's Beef Association representative who sat with his mouth agape as Oprah blurted out this now famous response, "It has just stopped me *cold* from eatin' another burger. I'm stopped!"

The impact of the broadcast was powerful and immediate. Panicked commodities traders anticipated a dramatic decline in

4

demand for beef; cattle futures plummeted, sending the market into a frenzy.

In a desperate attempt to restore the cattle industry's tarnished image, and to assuage the public's newest fears about the safety of America's food supply, Dr. Weber made a second appearance on the Oprah Winfrey Show the following week. But this time Mr. Lyman was not present to challenge Dr. Weber's assertions or to represent the public's interests. With major sponsors' interests at stake, this arrangement was disappointing, but not surprising. Nonetheless, it was too late for the cattle industry to fully recover: an outraged public had already gained new insight into what really lurks inside that sesame seed bun.

Prompted by this exposure and explosive media coverage of Britain's Mad Cow Disease fiasco, the FDA issued a long overdue final ruling on the practice of using mammal protein in animal feed in the United States. This seriously flawed 80-page regulation prohibits the feeding of rendered animal remains to cud-chewing ruminants, (i.e. cows), but exempts horses, pigs, chickens, fish, and pets. It also allows the continued use of swine, horse's blood, milk, and gelatin in animal feed, in effect leaving the public completely unprotected against transmissible spongiform encephalopathies (TSE'S).

Creutzfeldt-Jakob Disease (CJD), the human TSE form of Mad Cow Disease, accounted for at least eleven deaths in the U.K. CJD is an incurable and fatal degenerative brain disorder which closely resembles Alzheimers Disease. Victims suffer massive incoordination, seizures, and dementia preceding certain death. Yale and the University of Pittsburgh each conducted studies on the autopsied brains of Alzheimers patients. The findings: much higher than expected percentages of CJD in the U.S. population. Until such time that the FDA imposes a strict ban on ALL animal remains in ALL animal

....

feed, there is no way to ensure the meat-eating public's safety against the ravages of Mad Cow Disease.

Interest in vegetarianism is rising sharply as people continue to learn more about the personal and global implications of their dietary choices. An estimated 12 to 15 million Americans consider themselves vegetarian, and the number grows steadily by as much as a million each year.

After a Gallup poll showed that 20% of adults are likely to look for a restaurant that serves vegetarian items, the National Restaurant Association advised its members to feature a few vegetarian main-dish items on their menus. Even the Magic Kingdom has caught on to this trend. Veggie burgers are now being sold at Disneyland and Walt Disney World amusement parks. In fact, demand for the meatless patties has been continually rising since first being introduced in 1994.

Why do people decide to become vegetarians? Their answers vary. Some cite the atrocities that animals must endure even before they are slaughtered. Others are concerned about the harmful environmental effects of a meat-based diet, and many realize the impact that their food choices have upon world hunger. Millions are starving in third world countries while their grain is exported to fatten cattle to feed people in affluent nations. Still others eliminate meat from their diets simply because it is healthier. Heart disease, breast, prostate, and colon cancer, diabetes, stroke, osteoporosis and many other life-threatening illnesses are directly linked to meat-based diets. Texas Agriculture Department Assistant Commissioner Diane Smith, whose duties until recently included overseeing the marketing of beef, has her own reasons. Here's how she explains why she hasn't eaten meat in 14 years: "It has nothing to do with my work. It's a personal preference."

Some people change their eating habits overnight, while others make the transition to a more wholesome diet gradually.

Personally, there was not a moment's hesitation for me. After reading John Robbins' *Diet for a New America*, I never once looked back. But like most vegetarians I know, I was raised on a traditional American diet consisting mainly of meat and dairy products.

I grew up in New York City, under the guidance of two extremely doting parents. However, my mother hated to cook, which was fortunate for us because she wasn't very good at it, anyway. As a result, she saw to it that we ate out frequently, at least two or three times per week, an awful lot in those days. We'd frequently go to the neighborhood diner where I'd usually gorge on a bacon cheeseburger with French fries and onion rings, a coke, and top it all off with apple crumb cake a la mode, a napolean, or something equally sweet and gooey. I remember these occasions fondly, because they were a welcome retreat from my mother's disastrous attempts at preparing chopped steak or meatballs and spaghetti (made with butter and ketchup).

Breakfast was not exactly a nutritional haven, either. For my mom it consisted of coffee and a cigarette. For me, it was not much better, a Twinkie or Hostess Fruit Pie and secondhand smoke.

As I detested the taste of most luncheon meats, my mom usually packed the same thing for lunch everyday; cream cheese and jelly sandwiches on white bread with chocolate pudding for dessert. Could this diet have been the reason I was an overweight child?

This story may sound all too familiar if you grew up in the late fifties or early sixties; a time when most Americans were in total darkness about nutrition and health. But we can't blame our parents for their nutritional ignorance when the majority of family physicians knew even less. Today however, the overwhelming evidence in favor of a plant-based diet cannot be overlooked or ignored.

Whatever reasons you may have for choosing a vegetarian diet, this book is for you. Even if you still eat chicken or fish, chances are you know someone who is a vegetarian. Perhaps it's your teenager who arrives home from college with the unexpected news that she no longer eats meat, eggs, or dairy, leaving you to wonder what on earth you will feed her. (Warning: many vegetarian teens have been known to convert a parent or two.) Or maybe you've invited the boss over for dinner, and in the midst of preparing your famous Chicken Kiev, you receive an unexpected phone call from the boss's wife. She just wants to let you know that they are both strict vegetarians. Great, how do you make Kiev without chicken?

This book will make it simple for anyone to prepare and enjoy delicious plant-based meals in only a few minutes. There are no new complicated recipes to decipher, or expensive gadgets to buy. Within these pages you will learn about exciting new vegetarian foods with tastes and textures that are amazingly similar to the animal products they imitate but without the animal protein or cholesterol. Imagine meatless sausage, dairyless cheese and fishless tuna that look, taste and even smell much like their animal-based counterparts. Discover an incredible variety of burgers, burritos, and beverages made from nuts, grains, and tofu. Prepare your palate for tantalizing dishes made from exotic sounding ingredients like tempeh, seitan, and amazake.

The best part of all, is that thousands of healthful foods like these are readily available at your local natural foods store and many are even showing up on supermarket shelves. It's easier than you think. You just need know what to look for. So relax, turn the page, and take a journey with me into the exciting world of vegetarian convenience foods!

1

Getting Started:
A Fresh New Day

• •

*The gods created certain kinds of beings to replenish our bodies...they are
the trees and the plants and the seeds...*
- Plato

A diet comprised entirely of organic whole fruits,
vegetables, nuts, seeds, legumes, and grains is the ideal
sustenance for humans. But, as we navigate through our hectic
modern lives we often seek to find nourishment in foods that
are conveniently prepackaged and ready to eat. The delicious,
vegetarian food items listed in this book will fulfill that need.
However, I cannot stress strongly enough how important it is
that you include as many fresh, whole, organic fruits and
vegetables in your diet as possible. This is easily accomplished
by tossing a large, colorful vegetable salad and serving it along
with each meal, and by eating fresh, whole fruits throughout
the day. You might choose melon as an appetizer, berries for
dessert, and an orange, apple, banana, or peach as a snack.
    Although there is no human requirement for any foods of
animal origin, we have been influenced since childhood to think

....

otherwise. Through clever advertising campaigns directed at both children and adults, the meat, egg, and dairy industries have us convinced that without their products, we would hover on the brink of malnutrition.

From an early age, children are taught that without these foods, they will not grow big and strong. As adults, we continue clinging to this erroneous idea and unwittingly pass this belief on to our own children. Meanwhile, the media blitz continues, reinforcing the already ingrained nutritional lunacy. It is evidenced by the most frequently asked question of vegetarians: "But, *where* do you get your protein?"

That question is easily answered, but first, let's define vegetarian. A vegetarian diet excludes all meat products, such as beef, poultry, lamb, pork, and seafood. A person who eats chicken is *not* a vegetarian. (Although many people who eat poultry and fish may think of themselves as vegetarian.) A person consuming no animal flesh, but eating eggs and dairy, is referred to as a lacto-ovo vegetarian.

A strict vegetarian, or dietary vegan (pronounced vee-gun) has eliminated *all* products of animal origin from his or her diet including dairy, eggs, gelatin, and even honey. The foods listed in this book are predominantly vegan. The only two exceptions are foods containing honey (identified by an **h** symbol) and products containing casein (identified by a **c** symbol). Casein or caseinate refers to a milk protein present in many otherwise dairy-free foods. Manufacturers claim that using casein improves the taste, consistency, melting, and stretching properties of soy cheese and other products.

Protein

Vegetarians and vegans alike easily meet their protein requirement by eating a varied diet of vegetables, grains, and legumes. Consuming a variety of these foods sufficient to meet your caloric needs ensures that you will get enough protein in your diet. On the other hand, people who subsist on the Standard American Diet typically consume twice the amount of protein required by the human body. In case you are thinking that you cannot consume too much protein, bear in mind that excessive protein intake leads to osteoporosis and overworks the kidneys, liver, and digestive system.

Calcium

Many people wonder how vegans obtain their calcium. Although we have been led to believe that dairy products are the best source of this essential mineral, many plant foods provide the necessary calcium we need (without depleting it from our bodies at the same time.) Excessive protein intake depletes the body of calcium, so that when you drink a glass of milk, you later excrete the calcium in your urine. Contrary to popular belief, osteoporosis (wasting away of the bone tissue), is not a disease of calcium deficiency, but rather of calcium depletion. Dark, leafy, green vegetables are an excellent source of calcium. These include kale, collard greens, and spinach. Broccoli is also high in calcium as are soybeans, tofu, (particularly tofu made with calcium sulfate), tempeh, sesame seeds, figs, sea vegetables, molasses, and almonds. Many soy and rice milks are also fortified with calcium. One simple way to get calcium into your diet is to substitute dark leafy greens for lettuce (which has negligible nutritional value). Try using collard or other greens on a burger or sandwich, in salads, and shredded and sprinkled over cooked grains or pasta dishes. It's colorful, nutritious, and delicious.

....

Iron

Dark leafy greens also provide us with another essential nutrient, iron. Other iron-rich foods include dried beans, blackstrap molasses, and dried fruits such as raisins and figs.

Vitamins

A varied diet of vegetables, fruits, legumes, and grains contains bountiful quantities of Vitamin A (in the form of beta-carotene), vitamin C, and vitamin E. Exposure to sunlight ensures your body will manufacture all the vitamin D it requires.

The Recommended Dietary Allowance for vitamin B_{12} is only 2 micrograms per day. However, it can be a bit tricky to obtain on a vegan diet. B_{12}, necessary for healthy nerves and blood, is produced by bacteria naturally present in soil and water. Industrial agricultural practices have resulted in chemical pollution that has killed off many of these microorganisms. Eating vegetables freshly pulled from the ground and drinking water alone, will no longer guarantee us a sufficient supply of B_{12}. Because B_{12} is also present in the intestines of animals, carnivores and lacto-ovo vegetarians derive sufficient quantities of B_{12} from their diets. However, there is no reason to include animal products in your diet to get B_{12}. Reliable vegan sources of B_{12} include fortified breakfast cereals, soy milks, and rice beverages. Red Star Nutritional Yeast, which adds an appealing cheese-like flavor to foods, is also a great source of B_{12}. Another way to ensure you are getting this essential vitamin, is by taking a multi-vitamin or vitamin B_{12} supplements.

Cholesterol and Fat

All of the foods listed in this book are completely cholesterol-free. Many products are fat-free or low fat making these foods sound choices for a heart-healthy diet. Foods that are fat-free are identified by the ❤ symbol. Many recent scientific studies show that no more than 15% of our daily calories should come from fat and all health experts agree that the amount of fat consumed by the average American should be drastically reduced.

There are many completely vegetarian foods which are excluded from this book because they contain hydrogenated or partially hydrogenated oils. Unlike other vegetable oils, these oils are high in saturated fat. When you eat foods containing artery-clogging hydrogenated oils, your body responds by producing cholesterol. You may as well eat lard!

Hydrogenated oils are liquid oils that have been chemically altered to be solid at room temperature. Manufacturers use them because they are cheap, have a long shelf life, and add a smooth texture to foods. Products containing any of these oils should be avoided. Also, beware of products containing soy margarine. They usually contain hydrogenated soybean oil, although it may not be listed on the product label as such.

So, What's for Breakfast?

You'll find that when you are transitioning to a vegetarian diet, breakfast is the most effortless meal of the day. Without even realizing it, you are probably already eating mostly vegetarian food for breakfast. The best breakfasts include fruit. You can quickly blend a fresh fruit smoothie, (see the recipe on page 23) or top any cold or hot cereal with sliced bananas, raisins, or berries. There is an abundance of packaged multi-grain cereals to choose from, over which you can pour one of the many dairy-free alternatives to cow's milk listed in Chapter 2. Granola is another delicious option; just watch out for the fat content. Choose low fat varieties when you shop for granola. Hot cereal choices include, oatmeal, farina, cream of wheat, and delicious multi-grain varieties made from various combinations of rye, barley, buckwheat, and rice.

Two wonderful breakfast standbys are hearty whole grain toast, and bagels topped with a dollop of fruit-only preserves (see p. 68), a schmear of cream cheese alternative (see p. 29), or Spectrum Spread (see p. 69). Bagels now come in so many creative varieties, it's hard to choose. I usually enjoy my bagels plain and untoasted. After all, what do you really need to add to a banana walnut bagel? It's a complete eating experience all by itself! Once only found in places like New York and Chicago, almost every county across America now boasts at least one bagel bakery. Just stay away from the egg bagels and if you're not sure of the ingredients, ask the bagel baker.

For the more adventurous, there are many wonderful recipes for vegan muffins, scrambled tofu, pancakes, waffles, and even french toast. For those of you ready to take the next step in your vegetarian evolution and begin exploring fun and exciting recipe ideas, I highly recommend *The Peaceful Palate* by Jennifer Raymond, published by Heart & Soul Publications. Within its pages you will find a delightful collection of delicious, low fat, and simple to prepare vegan recipes.

Product Labels

ALWAYS READ PRODUCT LABELS! I cannot over stress this point. In addition to checking the nutritional value of the item, be sure to read the listed ingredients. There are many foods excluded from this book because they contain products derived from animals or hydrogenated oils. You may go shopping and discover that I have not listed a particular flavor or variety in a given product line. Careful inspection of the label may reveal the inclusion of an objectionable ingredient in that flavor or variety. Ingredients to watch out for in otherwise healthy sounding vegetarian food items include: whey, butter, milk solids, hydrogenated or partially hydrogenated oil, soy margarine, (usually contains hydrogenated soybean oil), gelatin, anchovies, and egg whites (which may also be listed as "albumin").

Where Do I Buy It?

IF YOU CAN'T FIND IT, ASK FOR IT! Most of the products you'll learn about in this book will be readily available at your local natural foods store. Supermarkets are beginning to stock natural food items in an effort to recover some of the consumer dollars lost to the growing number of health food stores throughout the country. A few food companies which traditionally catered to traditional American dietary tastes, have expanded their product lines to include healthy, vegetarian alternatives. These products, like Green Giant's Harvest Burger for Recipes™ are only found in supermarkets. If you cannot find a particular item, seek out the store manager or buyer for that item. More often than not, the store will do everything in its power to accommodate special requests to bring in an item. The best way to get a product you want into a store, is simply to ask for it.

In some cases, a store may not be able to get a special request item in house. They may not have the proper distribution channels in place to obtain the product, or in the case of some natural foods store chains, their corporate policy may determine that the item does not meet with their internal guidelines.

To the right of each product entry in this book, you will find the name of the company that manufactures, imports, or distributes the product. At the back of the book is a supplier's index which lists the name, address, and phone number of every company. You are encouraged to contact these suppliers directly if you are unsuccessful in obtaining a product at the store level. Manufacturers want to know if their products are not readily available to the customers who want them. They may even be able to direct you to a store in your area that carries the item you are looking for. Also, many suppliers provide retail mail order service and can ship products directly to you. These companies are highlighted in bold print.

If you are lucky enough to live within driving distance of a Trader Joe's market, I strongly urge you to discover this marvel of modern discount food shopping. Not only will you find many of the more popular items listed in this book at drastically reduced prices, but TJ's has an abundance of prepared vegetarian convenience foods manufactured under its own private label, including delicious fresh fruit smoothies and ethnic entrees.

Share Your Food Finds!

Exciting, new, completely vegetarian convenience foods are constantly being developed and introduced into the market. If you find a new item not mentioned in this book, and would like to share your discovery with others, please write and tell me about it. I'll be happy to include these products in subsequent editions of *So, Now What Do I Eat?* Please send product information to: Blue Coyote Press, P.O. Box 2101, Corrales, New Mexico 87048.

The most dangerous weapon in the arsenal of the
Homo sapiens is the table fork.

- Howard Lyman

The Difference Your Food Choices Make

Few of us realize the awesome power of our dietary choices. Just by consciously deciding to center our diets around plant-based foods we can drastically reduce our risk of heart disease, stroke, diabetes, osteoporosis, and breast, prostate, and colon cancers. We can help put an end to the extraordinary human suffering caused by hunger and malnutrition. We can effectively stop the senseless destruction of our world's rainforests which produce 80% of the Earth's oxygen. We can significantly impact our environmental concerns by reducing the toxic pollution of our air, soil, and water. Did you know that animal agriculture accounts for more pollution of our country's waters than all other sources combined? We can cut down on the thoughtless waste of these precious natural resources, which are not limitless. We can teach our children to become more loving and compassionate human beings by ceasing to raise them on the suffering of sentient creatures. Imagine...all of this power is just sitting there on the end of our forks!

Key to Symbols

♥ Fat Free
☆ Author's Favorite
❀ Kid's Pick
c Contains casein or caseinate
h Contains honey

2

Dairy Substitutes: Moove Over Milk!

. . . .

There is no biological need for milk.
- Suzanne Havala, M.S., R.D.
American Dietetic Association's
Position Paper on Vegetarian Diets

Milk

Soy, rice, almond, and oat beverages are all delicious alternatives to cow's milk. They're available in several flavors, with fat free and enriched versions. Most are packaged in aseptic cartons (known as Tetra Paks®), and have a shelf life of about one year. Once opened, they require refrigeration. Soy milks will then last about a week, while rice and almond beverages will last up to 10 days. Newer to the market are powdered versions of these beverages. They're a real lifesaver when traveling, since they come in small, easy to carry packages and you can mix only as much as you need.

Soy milks are thick and creamy and have a rather strong, distinctive taste. They are wonderful for making exotic coffee

18

drinks, shakes, and for use in all types of recipes. Chocolate soy milk is absolutely delicious. Kids adore it, and so do I.

Rice milk has a lighter consistency much like 2% dairy milk and is generally lower in fat. Vanilla rice milk is delicious in coffee drinks, poured over cereal, or enjoyed straight out of the carton.

Almond milk and oat milk each boast a unique flavor. They're completely versatile and tasty as beverages, poured over cereal, or added to recipes.

Soy Milk

EdenSoy®   Eden Foods, Inc.
Rich, creamy taste in
Original, Vanilla, or Carob.
EdenSoy® Extra
Fortified with antioxidants,
vitamins, and minerals in
Original and Vanilla.
Soy-Um™   First Light Foods
Rich, creamy taste in Original,
Vanilla, or Chocolate❀☆.
Soy Supreme™   The Hain Food
Original and Vanilla.   Group, Inc.
Fat-Free Soy Moo♥   Health Valley Foods
Great tasting; flavored with
vanilla.
So Nice™ Soymilk☆   International ProSoya
So much great taste in fresh   Corp.
(refrigerated) or Tetra Pak
cartons. You'll be amazed at
how much like dairy milk the
Original flavor tastes! If you

enjoy the taste of moo-milk,
this product was made just for
you. Natural, Vanilla Lowfat,
Original Low Fat, and Chocolate.

<u>Pacific Original Non-Dairy Beverage</u>   Pacific Foods
Unsweetened and Honey Vanilla**h**.   of Oregon, Inc.
<u>Pacific Select</u>
Low fat, low sodium beverage for
price conscious shoppers in
Plain or Vanilla .
<u>Pacific Lite</u>
1% fat in Plain, Vanilla, and Cocoa.
<u>Pacific Ultra-Plus</u>
Fortified with vitamins and L.
Acidophilus and L. Bifidus to
aid in digestion. Plain and Vanilla.

<u>Better Than Milk?</u>®   Sovex Foods, Inc.
Real dairy taste in Plain and
Vanilla**c**.

QUICK TIP: PERK UP HOT BEVERAGES!

Instead of adding cream and sugar to coffee, (refer to Chapter
10 for great coffee substitutes) or milk and honey to tea, stir
in vanilla soy milk. It's a sweet and delicious alternative to
traditional hot beverage additives. It's perfect for making
* latte and cappuccino drinks, too.

<u>Vitasoy</u>®   Vitasoy, Inc.
Original, Vanilla, Carob
Supreme, and Cocoa✿.
<u>Vitasoy® Light</u>
Only 1% fat in Original,

Vanilla, and Cocoa.

Westsoy® Organic   Westbrae Natural Foods
33% more protein than milk.
Original and Unsweetened.

Westsoy® Plus
Fortified with calcium, vitamins
A and D, and riboflavin.
Plain, Vanilla, and Cocoa✿.

Westsoy® Lite
Only 1% fat in Plain, Vanilla,
or Cocoa.

Westsoy® Non Fat♥
Plain and Vanilla.

Westsoy® Soy Drink
Made with malted cereal extract
containing barley; has less sugar, but
the same great taste as other Westsoy
milks. Available in Plain and Vanilla.

Westsoy® Concentrate
Economical, makes 2 quarts.
Plain and Vanilla.

Westsoy® Original Malteds
These refreshing dessert beverages in
handy single serving packages don't
really taste like malteds, but they're
rich and satisfying. Vanilla, Cocoa-
Mint, Almond, Java, and Carob.

Westsoy® Lite Malteds
Half the fat and 1/3 fewer calories.
Vanilla Royale, Cocoa-Mint,
Almond, Creamy Banana, and
Carob.

Silk™   White Wave, Inc.

Delicious tasting, Vanilla flavored
soy milk. Found fresh in your
grocer's dairy case.
<u>Chocolate Silk</u>❀✩
Fresh tasting chocolaty flavor.

Rice Milk

<u>Harmony Farms™ Fat-Free Rice Drink</u>♥   American Natural Snacks
Original and Vanilla.
<u>Rice Magic</u>   First Light Foods
Original and Vanilla.
<u>Rice Supreme™</u>   The Hain Food Group, Inc.
Original and Cinnamon.
<u>Rice Dream®</u>   Imagine Foods, Inc.
The original light, refreshing
rice beverage. Original, Vanilla✩,
Carob, or Chocolate❀.
<u>Rice Dream® Enriched</u>
Fortified with calcium and
vitamins A & D. Original,
Vanilla✩, and Chocolate❀.
<u>Pacific Lowfat Rice Drink</u>   Pacific Foods of Oregon, Inc.
Plain, Vanilla, and Cocoa.
<u>Pacific Fat Free Rice Drink</u>♥
Plain, Vanilla, and Cocoa.
<u>Westsoy® Rice Drink</u>   Westbrae Natural Foods
Plain and Vanilla.
<u>Rice Silk™</u>   White Wave, Inc.
Great fresh taste in the grocer's
dairy case (refrigerated).
<u>Westsoy® Rice Drink Concentrate</u>
Economical, makes 2 quarts in

Plain and Vanilla.

Rice & Soy Blend

EdenBlend® Rice & Soy Beverage   Eden Foods, Inc.
Blended rice and soy creates a
delicate balance of flavors.

QUICK TIP: BREAKFAST SMOOTHIE OF CHAMPIONS
Combine one cup of your favorite "milk" beverage with one
ripe banana, 1/2 cup frozen strawberries, and 1 tsp.
sweetener in a blender. Mix on high for a sensational
morning eye-opener.

Amazake

Amazake is a thick, rich, highly energizing beverage. It's
made by mixing organic brown rice with koji (a rice culture).
Fresh, cold Amazake tastes like a delicious dairy-free
milkshake. Use it as a base for desserts, puddings, sauces, and
smoothies. Amazake is naturally sweet (no added sugar) and
easily digestible. Find fresh Amazake in the your natural foods
store's refrigerator case, and a lighter, shelf stable version in
Tetra Pak® cartons.

Grainaissance Amazake   Grainaissance, Inc.
This beverage is so rich and
delicious, it should come with
a warning label that says, "Caution:
highly addictive." Fresh flavors are:

Original♥, Hazelnut, Almond Shake☆,
Cocoa-Almond❀☆, Sesame, Peanut
Butter❀, Apricot♥, Vanilla-Pecan,
Mocha-Java, Almond Light, Banana
Smoothie♥❀, Rice Nog☆, and Coffee.
Tetra Pak® flavors are: Original♥,
Almond Light, and Original Light♥.

QUICK TIP: FROZEN TREAT FOR BIG & LITTLE KIDS
Fill a popsicle maker with any flavor of Amazake. Freeze to
enjoy a great refreshment on a hot summer day!

Almond Milk

Naturally Almond   Pacific Foods of
Made from real almonds,   Oregon, Inc.
without added oils. Naturally
great tasting. Original and
Vanilla❀☆.

Oat Milk

Mill Milk   Nordic Farmers
This exciting new product from
Sweden combines organic whole
oats and canola oil for a fresh
and delicious non-dairy alternative.
Original and Vanilla☆.
Naturally Oat Non-Dairy Beverage   Pacific Foods of
Original and Vanilla.   Oregon, Inc.

....

Multi Grain Beverage

<u>Multi Grain Non Dairy Beverage</u>   Pacific Foods of
With triticale, oats, barley, soy   Oregon, Inc.
beans, brown rice, and amaranth.

Powdered Non Dairy Beverages

<u>Equi-Milk</u>❤   Equinox International
Refreshing taste, formulated with
potato extracts, fructose sweetened,
and supplemented with vitamins
and minerals.
<u>Heaven on Earth Fat Free Milk Replacer</u>❤   Lumen Foods
Tofu drink mix in Original and Carob.
<u>Riceness®</u>❤   Modern Products, Inc.
Original, Vanilla, or Chocolate.
<u>Soyness®</u>
Original, Vanilla, or Chocolate.
<u>Solait</u>   Sovex Natural Foods, Inc.
Soy based beverage mix in
Plain, Vanilla, and Chocolate.
<u>Better Than Milk?</u>
Tofu drink mix in Plain,
Plain Light, European Vanilla[c],
Carob, and Chocolate.
<u>Rice Moo</u>❤
Original or Vanilla.

Non Dairy Creamer

<u>Westsoy® Lite Non Dairy Creamer</u>❤   Westbrae Natural
50% less fat and 50% fewer calories   Foods

than half and half. Great in coffee drinks, over fruit, and on cereal.

Cheese

Many vegetarians are unaware that most dairy cheese substitutes contain casein or caseinate, a protein derived from cow's milk. Manufacturers add casein to soy and otherwise dairyless cheeses to make the product stretch and melt when heated. Although foods containing casein are free of lactose and cholesterol, they cannot be considered completely plant-based because casein is an animal product. The ^c symbol indicates that the product listed contains casein or caseinate.

Soya Kaas®^c   American Natural Snacks
Mozzarella, Monterey Jack,
Garlic & Herb, Mild American
Cheddar, and Jalapeno Mexi-Kaas.
Soya Kaas® Fat Free^{c♥}
Cheddar and Mozzarella.
Soya Kaas® Grated Soy Cheese^c
Parmesan flavor.
Vegie Kaas®
Casein-free spreads in Cheddar
and Smoked Cheddar flavors.
Nu Tofu® Cheese Spreads^c   Cemac Foods Corp.
Cream Cheese, Cheddar, and
Garlic & Herb.
Nu Tofu® Hard Cheeses^c
Mozzarella, Monterey Jack,
Cheddar, Jalapeno, Low
Sodium Mozzarella, and
Low Sodium Cheddar.

Nu Tofu® Fat-Free Cheeses^{C❤}
Mozzarella, Cheddar, and
Monterey Jack.
Lisanetti™ Brand Soy-Sation®
and Soy-Sation Lite^C
Excellent taste and texture.
Mozzarella, Jalapeno Jack,
Cheddar, and Garlic & Herb.
Lisanetti™ Almond Cheeze^C
Mozzarella, Pepper Jack,
Cheddar, and Garlic & Herb.
TofuRella and TofuRella Slices^C
Made with tofu in five flavors:
Cheddar, Mozzarella,
Jalapeno Jack, Monterey
Jack, and Garlic & Herb.
HempRella^C
Jamaica Jack flavor made
from hemp nectar.
Zero-fatRella^{C❤}
Tofu based in Cheddar,
Mozzarella, and Jalapeno
Jack.
AlmondRella^C
Made from almond milk:
Cheddar, Garlic-Herb, and
Mozzarella.
VeganRella
Made from Organic Rainforest
nectar (Brazil nuts) and boasting
a unique, nutty flavor. Two cream
cheese varieties: Plain and Onion
& Dill. Two semi-hard cheese

P.J. Lisac &
Associates, Inc.

Sharon's Finest

selections: Italian and Mexican.

Soy A Melt Soy Cheeses^C   White Wave, Inc.
Monterey Jack, Jalapeno, Garlic
Herb, Cheddar, and Mozzarella.
Soy A Melt Fat Free Soy Cheeses^{C♥}
Mozzarella and Cheddar.

Soyco Foods manufactures four different lines of cheese products. *Garden Accents* is made from soy as are *Lite & Less* cheese slices which contain less fat. The *Rice* line is soy-free and made from a rice beverage. Finally, *Soymage* cheeses are 100% vegan and casein free.

Grated Cheese

Garden Accents™^C   Soyco Foods
Caeser's Italian Salad, Parmesan,
Baked Potato, Cheddar, and Cajun.
Lite & Less™^C
Parmesan flavor.
Rice™ Parmesan^C
Soymage™ Parmesan☆

Chunk Cheese and Cheese Slices

SoySingles™^{C♥}
Mozzarella and American styles.
Lite & Less™ Veggie Slices^C
American❀, Swiss, Mozzarella,
Pepper Jack, and Provolone.
Rice™ Slices and Chunks^C
American, Mozzarella, and
Cheddar.

Soymage™☆
Mozzarella, Cheddar, Jalapeno,
and Italian Herb Chunk.

Soft Cheese

Soymage™ Chubs
Little logs of cheesy flavor in
Mozzarella and Cheddar styles.

Cream Cheese

Soya Kaas™ Cream Cheese^C☆   American
Creamy texture in Plain, Garlic &   Natural Snacks
Herb, and Garden Vegetable flavors.
Rice™ Low Fat Cream Cheese^C☆   Soyco Foods
Soymage™ Low Fat Cream Cheese

Sour Cream
Soymage™ Sour Cream
100% dairyless and tastes great!
Rice™ Low Fat Sour Cream^C

Yogurt

Hearty Life™ Instead of Yogurt™♥☆❀   Sovex Foods, Inc.
Phenomenally creamy, smooth,
rich taste. Just add water and
refrigerate. Slim, convenient
packages are great for travel.
This is vegan heaven!
Raspberry, Lemon, Pina
Colada, Peach, and Cherry.

....

Nancy's Soy Yogurt Treats**h**   Springfield Creamery
Contain active yogurt cultures
and honey. Plain, Blackberry,
Blueberry, and Strawberry.
Dairyless Soy Yogurt   White Wave, Inc.
Organic Plain, Raspberry, Lemon,
Strawberry, Blueberry, Peach,
Lemon-Kiwi, Banana-Strawberry,
Key Lime, Apricot-Mango, and Vanilla.

Key to Symbols

- ♥ Fat Free
- ☆ Author's Favorite
- ❀ Kid's Pick
- **c** Contains casein or caseinate
- **h** Contains honey

3

Soups and Canned Foods: Souper Simple Meals

. . . .

How good it is to be well-fed, healthy, and kind,
all at the same time.
- Henry Heimlich, M.D.

Soups

Healthy, delicious, vegetarian soups are widely available in cans, cups, cartons, and convenient, slim packages. Included here, are soups that are low-fat or completely fat-free and have passed rigorous taste testing to screen out the bland and the ordinary. Many soups are hearty enough to make a complete meal by themselves, (as are all of the chilis). But since you need not live by soup alone, you can toss a salad of fresh greens and raw vegetables, serve with a hunk of crusty whole-grain bread, and enjoy a wholesome, nutritious, and satisfying meal in minutes.

Dr. McDougall's Soups☆   Dr. McDougall's
Great tasting, low fat soup in   Right Foods, Inc.
a cup. Minestrone & Pasta, Split
Pea with Barley, and Tortilla Soup
with Baked Chips❀.
Ramen Noodles☆❀
Baked, not fried!
Completely vegetarian.
Chicken and Beef flavors.
Energy Cup Instant Meals☆
Tamale Pie with Baked Chips❀,
Pinto Beans & Rice, Southwestern
Style Pasta with Beans, Chicken
Flavor, and Mediterranean Style
Rice & Pasta Pilaf.
Shari's Bistro™ Organic Gourmet Soups   Fair Exchange
Canned soups with international flair: Inc.
Spicy French Green Lentil♥, Italian
White Bean with Herb**h**, Mexican Bean
Burrito, Indian Black Bean & Rice, Great
Plains Split Pea**h**♥, and Tomato with
Roasted Garlic**h**♥.
Fantastic Foods Hearty Soup Cups   Fantastic Foods,
Jumpin' Black Bean, Split Pea, Cha   Inc.
Cha Cha Chili☆, Country Lentil,
Couscous with Lentils, Five Bean,
and Vegetable Barley.
Fantastic Foods Couscous Cups
Black Bean Salsa, Creole Vegetable,
and Sweet Corn☆.
Fantastic Foods Only a Pinch Soup Cups
Couscous with Lentils and Spanish Rice
and Beans.

Fantastic Ramen Noodles Soup Cups
Chicken Free, Vegetable Curry, Vegetable
Miso, and Vegetable Tomato.

Geetha's Gourmet Dal Lentil Soup❤   Geetha's Gourmet
Truly thick and hearty with the   Products
savory flavors of India.

Organic Soups**h**❤   Health Valley Foods, Inc.
These canned soups are also
available in No Salt Added
versions: Minestrone, Potato
Leek, Lentil, Tomato, Vegetable,
Black Bean, Split Pea, and
Mushroom-Barley.

Fat-Free Healthy Soup In A Cup❤
Spicy Black Bean with Couscous,
Chicken Flavored Noodles with
Vegetable (no chicken), Zesty
Black Bean with Rice, Lentil with
Couscous, and Garden Split Pea
with Carrots.

Fat-Free Soup**h**❤
Canned soups: Vegetable Barley, Split Pea
and Carrots, Country Corn & Vegetable,
Black Bean & Vegetable, Lentil & Carrots,
5 Bean Vegetable, 14 Garden Vegetable,
and Tomato Vegetable.

Fat-Free Carotene Soup**h**❤
Contains 25,000 IU of beta-carotene.
Vegetable Power, Italian Plus, and
Super Broccoli in cans.

American Prairie Bean Soups   Mercantile Food
99% Fat free and made with   Company
organic ingredients. Vegetable

....

Bean, Black Bean, Split
Pea, and Lentil in cans.

American Prairie Cream Soups
Dairy-free, low-fat canned soups
made with organic veggies. Tomato**h**♥,
Mushroom, Potato Leek, or Broccoli .

Nile Spice™ Cups of Soup   Nile Spice Foods
Black Bean, Chili & Corn☆,
Lentil, Minestrone, Red Beans
& Rice, or Split Pea.

Chef's Classics® Instant Soups   Pacific Foods
Low-fat and flavorful soup cups.   of Oregon, Inc.
Black Bean, Minestrone, Savory
Lentil and Rice**h**, Cajun Red Beans
and Rice, Caribbean Black Beans
and Rice, and Curried Lentils & Rice.

Progresso® Lentil Soup☆   Progresso
Tasty and hearty canned soup.   Quality Foods Company

Ruthies Complete Vegetarian Meals   Ruthies Foods
Hearty and filling complete meal
dishes in convenient boil-in-bags.
Chili, Black Beans & Rice, Split Pea
Soup, Adzuki Beans & Rice, Lentils &
Rice, and Garbanzo Surprise.

Casbah® Teapot Soups   Sahara Natural
These tasty soups come in thin,   Foods, Inc.
convenient packages. Great for
traveling or camping. You provide
the cup and save money, too. Santa Fe
Rice & Beans, Hearty Lentil, Chicken
Noodle (no real chicken), Sweet Corn
Chowder, Garden Couscous, Vegetarian
Chili, Milano Minestrone, Potato Leek,

Split Pea, and Black Bean.

The Organic Gourmet™ Soup Bases♥   Scenario
For a hearty soup, just add your   International, Inc.
favorite vegetables or use alone for a
light, satisfying broth. Also make great
bases for gravies. Wild Mushroom Soup
'N Stock, Vegetable Soup 'N Stock, and
Vegetable Bouillon Cubes.

Quick and Natural Soups   The Spice Hunter
Delicious cup soups with flavors
from around the world. Brown &
Wild Rice Almandine, French
Country Lentil, Kasba Curry,
Mediterranean Minestrone, and
Moroccan Couscous.

Tradition Lowfat Ramen Noodle Soup☆   Tradition Foods
Wow! A great tasting and economical   Inc.
ramen soup without added MSG or
hydrogenated oils and only 1/2
gram of fat per serving. Find it in
the kosher section at your supermarket. In Oriental Style flavor.

Fat Free Soups of the World♥   Westbrae
Canned Hearty Milano Minestrone,   Natural Foods
Alabama Black Bean Gumbo,
Louisiana Bean Stew, Santa Fe
Vegetable, Great Plains Savory
Bean, Old World Split Pea, and
Rich Mediterranean Lentil.

Taste Adventure Soups   Will-Pak Foods, Inc.
Homemade taste in stay-fresh
multiple-serving cartons. Split
Pea, Black Bean, Curry Lentil,

....

Minestrone❀, and Navy Bean❤.

Chili

Greene's Farm® Vegetarian Chili**h**☆❀   Greene's Farm
Great tasting organically grown
3-bean chili in a can.

....

QUICK TIP: POTATO TOPPERS

Here's the perfect idea for leftover soup and chili. Store in
refrigerator until ready to use. Bake some potatoes (4-8
minutes in microwave on high). Top potatoes with
reheated soup or chili and serve!

....

Fat-Free Chili**h**❤   Health Valley Foods,
Fajita Flavor, Mild Vegetarian   Inc.
with 3 Beans, Mild Vegetarian
with Black Beans, or Spicy
Vegetarian with Black Beans.
No-Fat Added Chili**h**
Also available in No Salt Added.
Mild Vegetarian Chili with Lentils❤
Spicy Vegetarian Chili with Organic
Beans (only 1 gm. of fat), and Mild
Vegetarian Chili with Organic Beans❤.
Hormel® Vegetarian Chili with Beans❤   Hormel Foods
Flavorful chili loaded with kidney beans.   Corporation
Bearitos® Low Fat Premium Chili   Little Bear
Original, Spicy, and Black Bean.   Organic Foods
Stagg® 99% Fat Free Vegetable   Stagg Foods, Inc.
Garden™ Chili☆

Full of flavor four bean chili made
with a zesty variety of vegetables,
herbs and spices.

Taste Adventure Chili   Will-Pak Foods, Inc.
Homemade taste in stay-fresh
multiple-serving cartons--just
add water: Black Bean, Red Bean❊,
Lentil, and 5 Bean Chili varieties.

Baked Beans

Serve with veggie hot dogs, as a side dish to veggie cold cut
sandwiches, with barbecue tempeh, or over a bed of rice.

Bush's Best Vegetarian Baked Beans☆❤❊   Bush Brothers
The best vegetarian baked beans by far.   & Company
Fat-Free Honey Baked Beans**h**❤   Health Valley
Available in No Salt Added version.   Foods, Inc.
Contains Certified Organic Beans.

Refried Beans

A Mexican favorite. These vegetarian varieties are all made
without lard.

Shari's™ Refried Beans❤   Fair Exchange, Inc.
Black Bean, Pinto Bean, Pintos
with Roasted Garlic, Black Beans
with Roasted Red Jalapeño, Pintos
with Green Chili & Lime.
Rosarita® Vegetarian Refried Beans   Hunt-Wesson, Inc.
98% Fat Free Vegetarian, Low Fat
Black Bean, No Fat Traditional❤,

....

No Fat Zesty Salsa♥, and No Fat
Green Chile and Lime♥.

Bearitos® Low Fat Refried Beans   Little Bear Organic
Regular Pinto, Spicy Pinto, No   Foods
Salt, and Black Bean.

Bearitos Fat Free Refried Beans♥
Regular, Green Chili, or Black Bean.

Rice and Beans

Fantastic Foods Rice & Beans Cups   Fantastic Foods,
Bombay Curry, Cajun, Caribbean,   Inc.
Northern Italian, Szechuan, and
Tex-Mex varieties.

Bearitos Beans and Rice   Little Bear Organic
Cajun Style**h**, Mexican Style,   Foods
and Cuban Style .

Key to Symbols

♥ Fat Free
☆ Author's Favorite
❀ Kid's Pick
c Contains casein or caseinate
h Contains honey

4

Traveling Fare:
Savory Snacks and Edibles
You Can Enjoy Anytime

• •

If it has eyes or runs away, don't eat it.
-William Keith Kellogg

Camping Foods

Camping foods are transportable meals you can take with you anywhere; they're not just for camping. You can bring them to the office, on a long airline flight or train trip, to your hotel room, on a bicycling or sailing excursion, and of course, when you go camping. These foods are lightweight and convenient. The most you'll need is access to heat and water. In addition to the foods you'll find in this section, the many cup and package soups listed in Chapter 3 are lightweight and convenient for traveling, as are the powdered "milks" and yogurt mixes listed in Chapter 2.

AlpineAire Foods™
Naturally good food for
the outdoor gourmet.
Perfect for camping and
backpacking, these fully
dehydrated foods are
completely vegetarian and
come in easy to carry,
lightweight packages:
Alpine Minestrone Soup
Apple Almond Crisp**h**
Apple Sauce with Cinnamon♥
Chili
Couscous
French Cut Green Beans Almondine
Garden Vegetables♥
GOT'M (Good Old Trail Mix)
Granola
Hash Browns and Greens♥
Macaroni-Vegetable♥
Macaroni-Whole Wheat♥
Mashed Potatoes, Instant♥
Mountain Chili
Multi Bean Soup
Mushroom Pilaf with Vegetables♥
Peaches, Diced♥
Peanut Butter Pouches
Pineapple Chunks♥
Pure Maple Syrup♥(Dried)
Santa Fe Black Beans and Rice
Spaghetti Marinara with Mushrooms**h**
Sweet Bell Pepper Combo♥
Wild Rice Pilaf with Almonds

AlpineAire Foods

Backpacker's Pantry no-cook Meals   Backpacker's Pantry
Just add boiling water to the stand up
pouches and a delicious hot meal is
ready in minutes.
Wild West Chili & Beans
Louisiana Red Beans & Rice
Thai Spicy Peanut Sauce w/ Rice & Vegetables
Katmandu Curry w/Lentils & Potatoes
Shanghai Rice w/Vegetables
Sicilian Mixed Vegetables❤
Green Beans Almondine
Diced Potatoes❤
Peas❤
Corn
The following dishes require
minimal preparation:
Spaghetti and Sauce
Peas and Carrots❤
Fruit Cocktail❤
Oatmeal w/Mixed Fruit
Freeze dried fruit selections
contain only fruit.
Strawberries❤
Peaches❤
"Ya Gotta Eat" Quick & Delicious   Uncle John's
HomeStyle Air-Dried Meals❤   Foods
Many of these 100% vegetarian great
tasting foods are labeled NO COOKING
REQUIRED. These dishes taste fine either
hot or cold. They're digestible without
additional cooking and are made without
added salt or preservatives. Perfect for
backpacking or anywhere (even at home)!

Salad World

Good for Yer Eyes Carrot Salad
'Cool Hand' Cuke's Salad

International

Desert Ratatouille
Sheik Yerbouti's Curried Vegetables with Cous-Cous
Cuban-Style Rice and Beans
Hurry Curry

Hearty Hiker Meals

Dancing Vegetables with Barley
Homeboy Posole!
Keep Your Chowder Dry Corn & Potato Chowder

Old Reliables

Cowboy Chili
Reddy Spageddi
London Fog Pea Soup☆

More Easy Travelin' Foods

Tamarind Tree - The Taste of India
The old world tradition of delectable
Indian cuisine in microwavable/
boilable trays accompanied by boil-in-
bag brown rice. Now when I'm out of
town with an Indian restaurant nowhere
to be found, or it's 4:00 a.m. and I get

The Tamarind
Tree, Ltd.

a craving for spicy Indian cuisine, I thank
the people at Tamarind Tree for thinking of me!
Alu Chole (Curried Garbanzos & Potatoes),
Channa Dal Masala (Golden Lentils with Vegetables),
Dhingri Mutter (Garden Peas & Sautéed Mushrooms),
Saag Chole (Tender Spinach & Garbanzos), and
Vegetable Jalfrazi☆ (Spicy Garden Vegetables).

For the Munchies

The best snacks are simple...fresh whole fruits, fresh cut
vegetables, nuts, seeds, trail mixes, or dried fruits and veggies.
A few companies have made an art out of drying fruits and
vegetables. They are included below. Also try air-popped
popcorn sprinkled with Spike Salt-Free Seasonings or
cinnamon.

Just Tomatoes™❤   The Just Tomatoes Company
Like the name says, just
tasty bits of vine-ripened,
hand-picked tomatoes.
Great added to salads!
Just Bell Peppers❤
Just Veggies❤☆
A wonderfully sweet
and crunchy snack of
carrots, corn, peas, bell
peppers, and tomatoes.
Eat it just like popcorn!
Hot Just Veggies❤
The added jalapeno will
make your tongue and
taste buds sizzle.

....

Clif™ Bars   Kali's Sportnaturals, Inc.
The natural energy bar
made with rolled oats and
packed with flavorful goodies.
Chocolate Chip☆, Crunchy
Peanut Butter, Real Berry,
Chocolate Espresso, Apple
Cherry, Dark Chocolate, Apricot,
and Chocolate Chip Peanut Butter
Crunch☆❀.
Kicks Bars❀
The natural energy snack for both
kids and adults! Peanut Butter
Chocolate Chip, Strawberry, and
Apple Cinnamon.
Green Papaya Energy Bars**h**☆   Papaya John's
Scandalously delicious, these
energy bars are a blend of green
papaya with other fruits, nuts,
bee pollen, and papaya honey
concentrate.   One small slice
will give you an energy boost.
Papaya & Fruit, Papaya Fruit
& Ginger, Papaya Almond,
Papaya Macadamia Nut, and
Papaya Sesame.
Sonoma® Dried Fruits❤   Timber Crest Farms
With no preservatives or sulphur
added, these dried fruits make
wonderful snacks, can be sprinkled
on cereal and salads, or be used in a
wide variety of recipes. Persimmons,
Cherries, Figs, Cranberries, Blueberries,

Apples, Apricots, Peaches, Dates, Prunes,
Pineapple, Star Fruit, Papaya & Mango,
and Mixed Fruit.

<u>Sonoma Dried Tomato Bits</u>♥
Sprinkle on salads, or blend into
sauces and dressings.

<u>Sonoma Crystallized Ginger</u>♥
Spicy-sweet golden nuggets are
a refreshing nibble any time of
day.

Key to Symbols

♥ Fat Free
☆ Author's Favorite
❀ Kid's Pick
c Contains casein or caseinate
h Contains honey

5

Burgers 'n Dogs
'n Meat Analogues

• •

A few years ago, an obstinate friend of mine argued with me for hours on the pros and cons of eating meat (of course, there are no pros). I gradually gained ground and convinced him that the high-cholesterol, high-fat content of his carnivorous diet was clogging his arteries and leading him on the fast track to a heart attack. He even admitted to me once that he knew that hamburgers didn't *really* grow in hamburger patches. But, he continued to eat meat because he insisted that he just couldn't deprive himself of the "pleasure." Like a wish come true, my friend came to me one day and promised that he would give up meat for a week if I could recommend acceptable substitutes. That is how this chapter was born. Happily, now all the meats he eats are from this list.

Meaty Tasting Burgers

<u>Vegan Original Boca Burgers</u>™♥❀☆   Boca Burger
Textured like real hamburgers, and made   Company
from soy with a juicy, beefy, charcoal
grilled flavor. Kids love 'em. A favorite
at the White House and guaranteed to be
a favorite at your house.
<u>Ken & Robert's Veggie Burger</u>**c**   Imagine Foods
<u>Lightburgers</u>™❀   Lightlife Foods, Inc.
<u>NewMenu</u>™ Vegi~burger❀☆   Vitasoy, Inc.
Terrific tasting.
<u>Prime Burger</u>   White Wave, Inc.
<u>Morningstar Farms Better'n Burgers</u>♥   Worthington
Original style only (others contain   Foods, Inc.
egg whites).
<u>Natural Touch Vegan Burger</u>♥
<u>Yves Veggie Cuisine® Burger Burgers</u>♥❀   Yves Veggie
          Cuisine Inc.

Great Veggie & Grain Burgers

<u>Amy's Organic California Veggie Burger</u>☆   Amy's
Wonderful hearty flavor.   Kitchen Inc.
<u>Nature's Burger</u>   Fantastic Foods Inc.
Three unique great-tasting flavors:
Original Grilled, Roasted Red Pepper
and Garlic, and Southwestern Black
Bean☆.
<u>Mudpie® Veggie Burgers</u>   Mud Pie Frozen Foods
Straight from the menu of the famous
Mud Pie Vegetarian Restaurant in
Minneapolis come these delightful
burgers made from such wholesome

ingredients as brown rice, tahini,
fresh carrots, onions, oats, and millet.

Seenergy™ Vegetable Patties   Seenergy Foods Inc.
Loaded with spices and vegetables.
Mexican Style Fajita with Pinto
Beans, Thai Style Ginger with
Mung and Black Beans, and Texan
Style Ranch with Kidney Beans.

Sun's Veggie Light Patties   Sun Foods Ltd.
Delicious grain burgers. Choose from
Rice☆, Millet☆, Bean, and Falafel
varieties.

Superburgers™   Turtle Island Foods, Inc.
Juicy and full of flavor.
Original, BarBQ, and TexMex.

Veggie Life Burger   White Wave, Inc.

GardenBurger Veggie™♥c   Wholesome and Hearty
The one and only original.   Foods, Inc.

GardenVegan™♥☆
Same great taste without
the casein.

Yves Garden Vegetable Patties♥   Yves Veggie Cuisine Inc.

Tempeh Burgers

Marinated Grilles™   Lightlife Foods, Inc.
Soy-rice tempeh burgers drenched
in Barbeque, Tamari, or Lemon
Marinade.

The Soy Deli™ All-Natural Tempeh Burgers   Quong Hop
Delicious, precooked and ready in seconds.   & Co.
Original, Marinated, Hickory BBQ☆.

Sloppy Joe Tempeh❀

Tempeh Burger   White Wave, Inc.
Lemon Broil Tempeh Burger
Teriyaki Tempeh Burger

Tofu Burgers

Tofu burgers are traditionally high in fat. (Some get more than half of their calories from fat.) However, they are delicious and high in protein and other nutrients. When you do indulge, serve them on fat-free whole grain buns, along with a large, leafy green salad (with fat-free dressing), and oven-baked fries.

The Soy Deli All-Natural Tofu Burgers   Quong Hop
Made with tasty tofu, vegetables, sesame   & Co.
seeds, sunflower seeds, and currants.
Original, Garden, Teriyaki**h**☆, Texas
BBQ☆, Cajun Spice, Italian Spice,
and Garlic Veggie.
Tofu-Vegie™ Burgers   Wildwood Natural Foods
Made with tofu, onions, carrots,
and kale. Also in Mexican and
Italian styles.

Unique Burgers

Hempeh Burger   Sharon's Finest
Unusual flavor made from
nutrient rich hemp seeds.

Hot Dogs

Smart Dogs®❤   Lightlife Foods, Inc.
Taste just like hot dogs.

Tofu Pups®
Wonderdogs®❀
A milder taste just for kids.
SoyBoy® Leaner Wieners™❤   Northern Soy, Inc.
SoyBoy Not Dogs
Made with organic tofu.
SoyBoy Right Dogs
Oh, my dog!❀   Quong Hop & Co.
If nothing else, you gotta
love the name!
NewMenu™ VegiDogs❤   Vitasoy, Inc.
Meatless Healthy Franks   White Wave, Inc.
Meatless Jumbo Franks
GardenDog™❀   Wholesome and Hearty
From the folks who make   Foods, Inc.
Gardenburgers.
Wild Dogs❤   Wildwood Natural Foods
Yves Veggie Wieners❤❀   Yves Veggie Cuisine Inc.
Yves Tofu Wieners❤
Yves Jumbo Veggie Dog❤
It's really, really big!
Yves Chili Dogs❤☆
Nice spicy taste.

Meat Analogues

These meat-alikes are great in chili, spaghetti sauces, and tacos.
They also make fabulous pizza toppings.

Gimme Lean!™❤   Lightlife Foods, Inc.
Frozen ground meat substitute
requires prebrowning. Beef and
Sausage flavors.

Heartline™ Meatless Meats   Lumen Foods
Great tasting assortment of styles
have the look, taste, and texture of
a wide range of meats. Versatile and
easy to use. Requires no refrigeration.
Just boil or microwave in water for
15 minutes to reconstitute or snack on
them right out of the package! Plain
Unflavored, Beef Fillet, Ground Beef,
Canadian Bacon, Chicken Fillet,
Pepperoni, Italian Sausage, Mexican
Beef, Teriyaki Beef, and California Ham.
Heartline™ Lite
Lower in sodium and virtually no fat.
Beef Fillet Style, Ground Beef Style,
Canadian Bacon Style, Chicken Fillet
Style, and Pepperoni Style.
Green Giant® Harvest Burgers® for Recipes™♥☆   The
Tasty vegetable protein crumbles in clever   Pillsbury Co.
zip-lock packaging, prebrowned and ready
to eat. Find them in your supermarket's
freezer case.
Spice of Life Meatless Meats☆   The Spice of Life Co.
Easy, delicious, and versatile. Wide
assortment of meatless meats require
no refrigeration. Just add to boiling water
for 10 to 12 minutes (6 to 8 minutes in
microwave). Beef, Ground Beef, Mexican
Beef, Teriyaki Beef, Chicken, Chicken
Mince, Italian Sausage, Pepperoni,
Smoked Ham, and Unflavored.
Ready Ground™ Tofu   Tree of Life, Inc.
Readily substitutes for hamburger

....

in pasta sauces, chili, and much
more! Prebrowned; just add to
your favorite dish. Original☆,
Savory Garlic, and Hot & Spicy
varieties.

Nature's Ground™ Meatless❤   Vegenarian, Inc.
Requires some prebrowning. Three
zesty flavors: Italian Herb, California
Savory, and Mexicana Pepper. (frozen)

Morningstar Farms® Ground Meatless
All Vegetable Burger Crumbles❤☆   Worthington
Prebrowned and ready to eat. (frozen)   Foods, Inc.

Morningstar Farms Recipe Crumbles™
Textured vegetable protein and spices are
precooked and recipe-ready. In Burger Style
for use in tacos, sauces, and more. (frozen)

Natural Touch® Vegan Burger Crumbles™❤
Precooked vegetable and grain crumbles. (frozen)

Natural Touch Vegan Sausage Crumbles™❤
Adds zest to lasagna, casseroles, and
pizza. (frozen)

Yves Just Like Ground!❤☆   Yves Veggie Cuisine, Inc.
Flavorful precooked premium
meatless ground round. Ready to
eat, it comes refrigerated (not frozen)
for added convenience. In Original
and Italian varieties.

Sandwich Slices

Salami della Terra™☆   Della Terra, Inc.
Sensational deli slices made with
an old-world salami technique using

a unique combination of vegetables, fresh herbs & spices, wheat protein, soy sauce, and water. Whatever you have to do, get your hands on some of this stuff! In six outstanding flavors: Texas Barbecue, Southwestern Chili, Shiitake Mushroom, Yucatan Pepper, Sundried Tomato, and Italian Pepperoni.

Vegetarian Slice of Life™ from Vegi-Deli™ — Green Options, Inc.
Meatless Pepperoni in little sliceable logs. Tastes great alone, on a sandwich, or added to your favorite dishes. Ready to eat in Original, Zesty Italian, and Hot n' Spicy varieties.

Foney Baloney® — Lightlife Foods, Inc.
Tastes like bologna, and that's no baloney!

Smart Deli Thin Slices®♥
Country Ham, Roast Turkey☆, and Bologna style.

Longa Life™ Not Chicken™ — United Specialty Foods
Longa Life™ Not Ham™
Tender sandwich slices imported from Australia.

Meat Free™ Tender Deli Cuts™♥ — Soyco Foods
These delectable all vegetable slices boast a cheese-like consistency and a wonderful smoky flavor. In three styles: Hickory Smoked Turkey☆, Honey Smoked Ham☆, and Peppercorn Chicken.

Meatless Sandwich Slices♥☆ — White Wave, Inc.
Chicken, Turkey, Beef, or Pastrami.

....

Yves Deli Slices♥❀   Yves Veggie Cuisine Inc.
I never liked luncheon meat,
but I really do like these slices.

Sausage and Bacon

Lean Links Meatless Italian Sausage   Lightlife
The taste and texture of real Italian   Foods, Inc.
sausage.
Lean Links™ Meatless Breakfast Sausage
Meatless Lightsausages♥
Fakin' Bacon®☆
Delicious tempeh strips. Heat and serve with
scrambled tofu or use to make a BLT sandwich.
Maayo™ Natural Foods Vegetarian Chorizo™☆   Alcala
Used in Mexican and Spanish cooking,   Enterprises
chorizo is a highly seasoned, coarsely
ground sausage flavored with garlic, chili
powder and other spices. This vegetarian
version closely resembles the traditional
sausage right down to the casing! Remember
to remove the casing and crumble the chorizo
before adding to tofu, pasta, or rice dishes.
Maayo™ Natural Foods Vegetarian Romanelli™☆
In Italy, romanelli refers to the best meat available
in one's kitchen. By tradition, romanelli is saved
for honored guests and special occasions. As in
Italy, this vegetarian version is seasoned with
garlic, basil, and oregano. Remove the casing,
saute with onions, and crumble to add pizzazz
to any of your favorite dishes.
SoyBoy Vegetarian Breakfast Links   Northern Soy, Inc.
Green Giant® Breakfast Links   The Pillsbury Company

Nature's Ground Meatless
Gourmet Sausage♥   Vegenarian, Inc.
Succulent gourmet sausages even
have meatless skins! In Tomato Basil,
Tuscan Herb, and Spicy Andouille.
Yves Canadian Veggie Bacon♥☆   Yves Veggie
Enjoy the traditional taste of Canadian   Cuisine Inc.
bacon and rediscover the joy of an old-
fashioned breakfast.
Yves Veggie Pepperoni♥
Yves Veggie Pizza Pepperoni♥
Made especially to be used as
a pizza topping .

Seitan

Seitan's versatility comes from its firm, chewy texture
which makes it an ideal substitute for meat (especially chicken).
Also called wheat meat, seitan has a neutral taste. It easily picks
up the flavors of the sauces, spices, and other foods with
which it is cooked. The following seitan entries are ready to
eat and can also be used in a variety of dishes.

Savory Seitan™   Lightlife Foods, Inc.
Delicious entrees are easy to heat
and eat or slice and serve for great
hot or cold sandwiches. With Barbeque
Sauce☆ or Teriyaki Sauce.
Meat of Wheat Gourmet Grain Protein   White Wave, Inc.
Delicately seasoned, precooked tender
chunks are great for salads, kabobs,
sauces, and more. In Chicken Style,
Sausage Style, and Grilled Burgers.
Traditional Seasoned Seitan♥

Vegetarian Fajita Strips♥
Vegetarian Philly Steak Slices♥
Vegetarian Sloppy Joe

Snack Meats

Vegetable Jerky™♥   Garden of Eatin' Inc.
Smoky and chewy just like real
jerky, in 3 flavors: Hot n' Spicy
BBQ, Pepperoni Pardner, and
Western Roast.

Cajun Jerky   Lumen Foods
Beef, Hot Pepperoni, Spicy Italian,
and Smoked Ham.

Stonewall's Jerquee
In Mild and Wild styles.

All Natural BBQ™ Fib Rib☆   Nobull Foods
These spicy, savory snacks are
available in two varieties; one
sweetened with honey, one
sweetened with sugar. Check the
label. (Sugar-sweetened bears the
PETA Vegan Seal.) In four flavors:
Original, Hot'n'Spicy, Jalapeno,
and Oriental.

Spice of Life™ Meatless Jerky☆   The Spice of Life Co.
The ultimate vegetarian snack
food. It's wonderfully delicious.

Chicken Substitutes

Chicken-Free Nuggets❋☆   Health is Wealth, Inc.
Made extra crispy, these tender

nuggets are low in fat and breaded
with stone ground whole wheat.
Superb new taste you can enjoy
with your favorite dipping sauce:
ketchup, barbecue sauce, honey
mustard, or sweet and sour sauce.
<u>Chick'n Burger</u>♥❀☆   White Wave, Inc.

Something's Fishy

<u>Tuno</u>❀☆   Worthington Foods, Inc.
Tuno tastes, looks, and smells so
much like tuna fish, the first time
someone offered it to me, I thought
it was real tuna and wouldn't eat it.
Since then, my fears have subsided,
and I've become a real Tunoholic.
Do with Tuno whatever you would
do with canned tuna. Mix it with a
little Nayonaise, celery, shredded
carrots, onions, or relish. Spread it
on whole wheat toast and add a little
leafy green lettuce and sliced tomato.
Then get set for an incredible lunchtime
treat!

Key to Symbols

♥ Fat Free
☆ Author's Favorite
❀ Kid's Pick
c Contains casein or caseinate
h Contains honey

6

Dressings, Dips, Sauces, and Spreads to Relish

· ·

If we understand that the greatest act of devotion and worship to God is not to hurt or harm any or His beings, we are loving God.
- Meher Baba

Our health and well being are enhanced significantly when we eliminate meat, dairy, and eggs from our diets. But, it is just as important that we limit our intake of dietary fat. So, does that mean we have to give up rich tasting, dips, spreads, sauces and dressings? Absolutely not! Certainly, a fat is a fat is a fat, and as far as your waistline is concerned, one fat is as fattening as any other. Joyfully, many of the following condiments are completely fat-free or very low in fat and can be enjoyed frequently. Some items are high in fat, and should be used in moderation. However, all of the listings are free of unhealthful animal products, cholesterol, and hydrogenated oils. So, go ahead; pour, dip, schmear, and indulge yourself!

Chutney

These traditional condiments from India add zestful flavor to virtually any meal.

Earth/Sun Farm Chutneys   Earth/Sun Farm
Made from organic ingredients
grown in the small farming
community of Dixon, New
Mexico. The delicate flavors
of these chutneys will delight
your taste buds. Samadhi
Chutney**h**, Dixon Red Chile
Chutney**h**, Southwest Sunrise
Apricot Chutney**h**, Urie Gingered
Plum Chutney, and Exquisito
Piñon/Pear Chutney☆.

Essence of India™ Chutney♥☆   Essence of India, Inc.
Tomato Chutney is a provocatively
sweet, spicy relish. Raisin Chutney
is tangy, fruity, and wonderfully
delectable.

Geetha's Gourmet Chutney**h**♥   Geetha's Gourmet
Delicious Date & Raisin and Mango.   Products

Hawaiian Kukui® Mango Chutney   Hawaiian Fruit
With pineapples and assorted fruit   Specialties Ltd.
flavors.

Taj Creative Condiments☆   Taj Gourmet Foods
Tangy Tamarind Chutney, Sweet
Mango Chutney**h**, and Hot Mint
Chutney.

Dips

I used to think a dip could mean only one thing: sour cream and onion soup mix. Then, all you all you needed were the potato chips. Talk about a fat and cholesterol laden snack! Now I know better. Dips can be fun, tasty, healthful additions to any party or you can enjoy them when you just feel like being a couch potato. The following dips are cholesterol and fat free. Just add fresh, cut fruits or veggies or your favorite baked tortilla chips and enjoy a totally guilt-fee indulgence.

Organic Fat Free Bean Dips❤ Spicy Chipotle Red Bean☆, and Baja Black Bean.	Garden of Eatin', Inc.
Goldwater's taste of the southwest™❤ Paradise Pineapple Black Bean Dip.	Goldwater's Foods of Arizona
Guiltless Gourmet Fat Free Dips❤ Mild Black Bean, Spicy Black Bean☆, and Spicy Pinto Bean.	Guiltless Gourmet, Inc.
Bearitos® Fat Free Bean Dips❤ Pinto Bean, Black Bean Salsa, and Black Bean.	Little Bear Organic Foods
Saguaro No Fat Dips❤ Spicy Black Bean**h**, Spicy Pinto Bean**h**, and Guacamole. Also available under the Cool Coyote label at gift and gourmet food shops.	Saguaro Food Products

Salad Dressings

Blanchard & Blanchard® Vermont Classic Dressings Mustard Vinaigrette, Lemon Pepper	Blanchard & Blanchard Ltd.

Vinaigrette, All Natural Poppy Seed,
Honey Mustard Tarragon**h**, Toasted
Sesame Seed, Northern Italian, Garlic,
Tomato Basil, and Lemon Mustard Dill.
Blanchard & Blanchard® Vermont Fat
Free Dressings♥
Balsamic Tomato Herb, Balsamic Cracked
Pepper, and Balsamic Roasted Garlic.
Blanchard & Blanchard® Vermont Low
Fat Spa Dressings
Balsamic Italian, Balsamic Honey
Blackberry**h**, Honey Dijon**h**. Country
Italian, and Russian Tomato.
Briannas® Home Style Dressing   Del Sol Food Co., Inc.
Rich Poppy Seed☆, Dijon Honey
Mustard**h**, Blush Wine Vinaigrette,
Real French Vinaigrette, and Zesty
French.
Briannas Special Request Dressing♥
Lively Lemon Tarragon**h** and Rich
Santa Fe Blend☆.
Food For Living Dressings   Food For Living
In four creamy flavors: Garlic Dill,
Maple Mustard☆, Toasted Poppyseed,
and Ranch Style (has the tartness of
buttermilk without the dairy).
Straight Out 'the Garden® Dressings   Food From The
Delicious salad toppers from a natural   'Hood
food products company owned and
operated by inner city High School
students. Creamy Italian and Honey
Mustard♥☆.

....

Martin Brothers Distinctive Salad Dressings☆   Martin
Discover the vitality of the freshest of   Brothers Cafe
ingredients. Find these dressings in your
store's refrigerator case. Creamy Miso,
Tamari Vinaigrette, Garlic Mustard, and
Thai Peanut.

Spike Splashers!™ Vinaigrette   Modern Products,
From the makers of Spike Seasonings,   Inc.
three flavorful salad dressing and
marinade flavors. Splash them on
salads, stir fries, pasta, or rice dishes.
Original☆, Fat Free♥, and Salt Free.

Nasoya® Vegie-Dressing™   Nasoya Foods, Inc.
These creamy, full-bodied dressings
will perk up your favorite salad.
Creamy Dill, Sesame Garlic, Garden
Herb, Thousand Island☆, and Creamy
Italian.

Riverbank™ All Natural Dressings**h**   The Rainforest
Fresh spices from the banks of the   Company
Amazon River create these unique
tasting dressings. 10% of The
Rainforest Company's earnings
are donated to sustain the
rainforest and its peoples.
Lime Vinaigrette♥, Raspberry
Cashew☆, and Ginger Sesame.

Simply Delicious® Vinaigrette Un-Dressing   Simply
The secret to all the delicious flavor in these   Delicious, Inc.
un-dressings is Soy Gold™, a golden shoyu
made with whole grains and soybeans.
Lemon Tahini, Miso Sesame☆, Ginger
Plum**h**, Tofu Poppyseed☆, Honey Mustard**h**,

and Herb Garlic**h**.

herbalicious® Fat-Free Vinaigrette♥
Made with organic apple cider vinegar:
Garlic Italian, Dill Cucumber, Miso
Ginger, Tarragon Mustard**h**, Tomato
Basil**h**,and Roasted Pimento**h**.

Spectrum Naturals® Dressing & Marinade   Spectrum
Zesty Italian, Mango Madness**h**,   Naturals, Inc.
Sweet Onion & Garlic♥, and
Toasted Sesame.

Relish

When I discovered these relishes, I knew I had stumbled upon
something exciting. You'll adore their unique, zesty flavors.

Earth/Sun Farm Eggplant Newcamp**h**☆   Earth/Sun Farm
This wonderfully spicy, piquant relish
will add pizzazz to any dish.

Fiesta Olé Hot Relish**h**♥   Geetha's Gourmet
Try these relishes on salads, with   Products
crackers or chips, over your favorite
veggie hot dog or mixed with Tuno.
Hot Fruit and Hot Vegetable varieties.

Salsa

Not just for chip-dipping, experience the amazing variety of
salsas available. They're great for adding spicy flavor to stir-
fries, salads, rice, pasta, or scrambled tofu dishes.

Adeline's™ Gourmet Salsa♥☆   Adeline's Gourmet
Fruity and flavorful in three   Foods, Inc.

tantalizing varieties: Mango,
Kiwi, and Pineapple Guava.

Sorrel Ridge® Fruit Salsa♥   Allied Old English, Inc.
Boasts a fruity-tomato taste
in mild or medium strengths.
Peach, Orange Peel, and
Pineapple☆.

Coyote Cocina Salsa♥   Coyote Cocina
Created by world-famous chefs
at the Coyote Cafe in Santa Fe,
New Mexico. Four unique flavors:
Fire-Roasted☆, Roasted Corn &
Black Bean☆, New Mexico Green
Chile, and Flamin' Pineapple.

Organic Fat Free Salsa♥   Garden of Eatin', Inc.
Cha Cha Corn☆, Hot Habanero,
and Great Garlic Mild.

Fiesta Olé Salsa♥   Geetha's Gourmet
Thick and hearty in Green Chile   Products
Bean and Red Chile Bean.

Goldwater's taste of the southwest™   Goldwater's Foods
From subtle and fruity to fiery hot!   of Arizona
Sedona Red♥, Rio Verde Tomatillo♥,
Paradise Pineapple♥, Ruby Raspberry♥,
Sabino Strawberry♥☆, Mohave Mango♥,
Papago Peach♥, Sedona Red Hot♥, and
Cochise Corn and Black Bean☆.

Guiltless Gourmet Fat Free Salsa♥   Guiltless Gourmet,
Medium Salsa, Green Tomatillo,   Inc.
Roasted Red Pepper, and Southwestern
Grill.

Kukui Tropics Hawaiian Papaya Salsa♥   Hawaiian Fruit
Unusual, distinctive taste with just a   Specialties Ltd.

hint of curry.

Hawaiian Jungle Jazz Sweet & Sassy
Guava Salsa❤

R.W. Knudsen Family Fruit Salsa❤   Knudsen & Sons,
The sweetness of pineapple combined   Inc.
with peppers and tomatoes for a truly
unique taste. Available in two flavors:
Tomato & Pineapple and Pineapple &
Pepper. Mild☆ or Hot varieties.

Milagro™ Country Foods Salsa❤   Milagro Country
Spicy, hot, and delicious. Passion   Foods
Peach and Habanero Fiesta.

Newman's Own All-Natural Bandito Salsa❤   Newman's
All profits go to charity. Comes in Mild☆,   Own, Inc.
Medium, and Hot.

Riverbank Salsa   The Rainforest
Mango❤, Brazilian Red❤, Black Bean &   Company
Corn, and Tomatillo Chipotle.

Southwest Spirit™ Gourmet Culinary Salsa   RGE, Inc.
Rio Red Habanero with Dried Tomatoes.

Saguaro No Fat Salsas❤   Saguaro Food
Chipotle, Southwestern, and   Products
Santa Fe Harvest. Also available
under the Cool Coyote label at
gift and gourmet food shops.

Santa Barbara Award Winning Salsa   Santa Barbara
Made with the freshest all natural   Creative Foods, Inc.
ingredients, you'll find these salsas
in your market's refrigerator case.
Roasted Garlic❤, Salsa Verde, Black
Bean & Corn❤, Fire Roasted Chili❤,
Italian Olive, Mango❤, Hot❤, and Mild❤.

Santa Barbara Naturals Salsa
Same great flavor in shelf stable jars.
Mango♥☆, Garlic & Herb, Roasted
Garlic♥, Italian Olive, Black Bean
& Corn♥, and Roasted Chili♥☆.

QUICK TIP: SASSY SALAD DRESSING
For a delicious fat-free or nearly fat-free salad dressing, just
pour your favorite salsa over tossed raw veggies!

Sauces

Essence of India™ Sauces   Essence of India, Inc.
Bring home the savory flavors of
India with Bombay Mint Sauce♥
and Classic Curry Sauce.
Geetha's Gourmet Curry Sauces☆   Geetha's Gourmet
These thick, rich curries are   Products
packed with vegetables. Each
variety is truly a meal in itself.
Punjab Spinach or Vegetable Curry♥.
Hawaiian Kukui® Sweet Sour Sauce   Hawaiian Fruit
Zesty taste made with pineapples.   Specialties Ltd.
Holy Chipotle☆   Holy Chipotle
This wonderfully spicy sauce made
from chipotle peppers can be added to
any Mexican food, used as a marinade
or barbecue sauce, or simply be enjoyed
with chips.
Hunt's® Manwich® Sloppy Joe Sauce♥✿☆   Hunt-Wesson,
Fabulously, fun food! Just add your   Inc.

favorite ground meat substitute from
Chapter 5 and serve on whole wheat
buns. I prefer the Original flavor with
Green Giant Harvest Burgers for Recipes™.
Original, Bold, Barbecue, and Taco &
Burrito.

Heartline Sauces   Lumen Foods
Inaptly called sauces, these are complete
meals in a jar. Thick and meaty taste using
Heartline's Meatless Meats. Texas Chili,
BBQ Beef, and Spaghetti❀ varieties.

Ha Chi Wawa! Xtra-Hot Habanero Hot Sauce❤   Milagro
The name of this sauce says it all! Made with   Country
both Jalapéno and Habanero peppers.   Foods

Riverbank™ Cooking Sauces   The Rainforest
Exotic rainforest flavors add spice to   Company
tofu, tempeh, pasta, stir-fries and more!
Mulitas Marinade❤ (tangy, citrus Cuban
Marinade), Jamaican Jerk (smoky and
spicy), or Ginger Curry Stir Fry**h** (with
an Oriental accent).

Southwest Spirit™ Zia Fire   RGE, Inc.
This fiery hot sauce combines the fresh
flavors of habanero chile, garlic, peanut,
and pineapple.

Flavors of the Rainforest™   Simply Delicious,
Add exciting flavor to dishes with   Inc.
these new tropical condiments. Papaya
Pepper Tropic Hot Sauce**h**, Green
Habanero Hot Sauce**h**, Savory Spice
Everyday, Everyway Sauce**h**, Ginger
Curry Stir-Fry Sauce, Mango BBQ &
Grille Sauce**h**, and Five Pepper Sauce**h**.

Troy's® Natural Saucery
Savory sauces create wholesome
and natural international dishes.
Low Fat Peanut Sauce**h** (great for
Thai dishes), Low Fat Garlic Sauce,
Fat Free Curry Sauce**h**, Fat Free Jerk
Sauce**h♥**(for Caribbean flavor), Fat
Free Chipotle Sauce**h♥** (for Mexican
and Southwestern meals), and Fat
Free Ginger Sauce**h♥** (for noodles or
Oriental dishes).

Taj Simmer Sauces   Taj Gourmet
Heat and serve sauces create the exotic   Foods
flavors of India. Serve with vegetables,
or tofu, over rice, with chapati or pita
bread. Bombay Curry and Calcutta Masala.

Spreads

Sorrel Ridge® 100% Fruit♥❀☆   Allied Old English,
Spreadable fruit sweetened only   Inc.
with fruit juice concentrates.
Blackberry, Strawberry, Black
Cherry, Raspberry, Boysenberry,
Black Raspberry, Apricot, Wild
Blueberry, Peach, Concord Grape,
and Orange Marmalade.

Vegenaise® Dressing & Sandwich Spread   Follow Your
The taste of real mayonnaise without the usual   Heart
eggs, dairy, or refined sugars. Must be kept
chilled to maintain its creamy, whipped texture,
so look for it in your store's refrigerator case.
Original and Grapeseed Oil varieties.

Almonnaise   Food For Living
Unique, light, almond-based spread
is a wonderful base for creamy sauces.
Spread on bread when making your
favorite sandwiches or use for making
party dips.

Peanut Better❀☆   Mrs. Malibu
What's extraordinary about this peanut   Foods, Inc.
butter spread? It's 92% fat free! Now you
can have it all. Great peanut butter taste
and only 2.5 grams of fat per serving!

Nayonaise® Vegi-Dressing™ & Spread☆   Nasoya Foods,
Creamy, delicious eggless alternative   Inc.
to traditional mayonnaise.

Fat-Free Nayonaise Vegi-Dressing & Spread♥☆
Rich, full-bodied spread without the fat!
How did they do that?

Rice™ Low Fat Spreadᶜ   Soyco Foods
Boasts a thick, buttery flavor.

Spectrum Spread™☆   Spectrum
A marvelous tasting non-dairy,   Naturals, Inc.
non-hydrogenated, cholesterol-free
alternative to butter and margarine.

Natural Touch® Roasted SoyButter™❀☆   Worthington
Allergic to peanuts? Tired of nut butters   Foods
that separate and turn hard? Roasted
SoyButter has a rich, smooth, and
creamy texture. A wonderfully nutty
tasting alternative to peanut butter.

Key to Symbols: ♥ Fat Free ☆Author's Favorite ❀ Kid's Pick
ᶜ Contains casein or caseinate **h** Contains honey

7

Frozen Meals:
Chilling Surprises

· ·

Eating vegetables and tofu will keep you in peace.
- Chinese folk saying

Look inside my freezer and you will find an extraordinary assortment of international cuisine. I no longer feel that I have to eat out in order to take my palate on a trip to far-away lands. From the classical, to the exotic, there is an abundant selection of taste-tempting frozen foods to explore.

American Favorites

Non-Dairy Vegetable Pot Pie[h]   Amy's Kitchen Inc.
Shepherd's Pie
Macaroni & Soy Cheeze[c]❀
Veggie Loaf Dinner[h]
Cedarlane™ Low Fat Hearty Vegetable Stew[h]   Cedarlane
Chunks of carrots, peas, mushrooms, onions,   Natural
potatoes, and organic tofu in a savory country   Foods, Inc.
style gravy.

....

Farm Foods® Vegetarian Chili   The Hain Food
Three varieties to choose from: Group, Inc.
Six Bean, Read Bean, and
White Bean.

Indian Delights

Serve any of these flavorful dishes with the chutneys found in
Chapter 6.

Green Guru™ International Cuisine   Deep Foods, Inc.
Delicious Indian entrees: Channa
Masala (chick peas sauteed with onions,
tomatoes, and exotic spices), Vegetable
Biryani☆, (sauteed vegetables and tofu
with savory sauce and exotic spices), and
4 Naan Bread, (traditional whole wheat
bread is the perfect complement to Indian
cuisine).

Taj Gourmet Meatless Authentic Recipes☆   Taj Gourmet
Delicately spiced classic Indian entrees   Foods
served with organic rice pilau. Bean
Masala (a delightful bean and tomato
medley), Channa Bhajhi (sauteed chick
peas with fresh ginger, garlic and onions),
Raj Mah (kidney beans sauteed with ginger,
garlic, onions, and tomatoes), Eggplant
Bhartha (roasted eggplant and green peas),
Asparagus and Baby Carrots Subzi,
Mushrooms and Green Peas Masala, Dal
Bahaar (an aromatic blend of lentils and
garlic with carrots, green peppers and tofu),
and Vegetable Korma (a mixture of fresh

vegetables with ginger, garlic, tomatoes,
onions, cashews, and raisins).

Taj Gourmet Samosas**h**
Savory Indian turnovers that are baked,
not fried. Three zesty fillings to choose
from: Aloo (potato), Gobi (cabbage and
peas), and Subzi (mixed vegetables).

Jaipur Roti Express   Natural
Wheat tortillas filled with mildly   Life, Inc.
spiced curried Indian vegetables.
Try Bean Medley, Cauliflower
and Peas, Mixed Veggies☆, and
Bombay Potatoes with Onions.

Jaipur Baked Vegan Samosa
Savory pastries stuffed with peas,
potatoes, and mild spices.

Jaipur Entrees
Flavorful dishes served with Basmati
Rice Pilaf. Vegan Chili, Madras Lentils☆,
Punjab Chick Peas, Lima Beans and
Veggies, and Vegetable Melange☆.

International Foods

Cascadian Farm® Meals For A Small Planet™   Cascadian
Organic vegetarian meals with an international   Farm
flair. Cajun, Oriental, Aztec, Moroccan☆,
Mediterranean, and Indian.

Cascadian Farm® Organic Veggie Bowls™
Szechuan Rice, Teriyaki Rice, or Pasta
Marinara.

Vegetarian Request® Meals   Lightlife Foods,
Seven classic recipes: French Country Stew,   Inc.

Moroccan Lentil Stew, Tuscan White Bean
Stew, Penne Pasta Bolognese, Thai Tofu,
Vegetable Croquette Dinner, and Traditional
Meatloaf.

Italian Classics

Tofu-Vegetable Lasagna   Amy's Kitchen Inc.
Celentano® Vegetarian Selects☆   Celentano
Delizioso! Non-Dairy Eggplant
Rollettes, Non-Dairy Lasagna
Primavera, Non-Dairy Spinach
& Broccoli Manicotti, and Non-
Dairy Spinach & Broccoli Stuffed
Shells.
Hain Pure Foods® Vegetarian Classics   The Hain Food
Radiatore Bolognese (cooked pasta in   Group, Inc.
marinara sauce).
Legume® Fine Vegetarian Cuisine   HKS Marketing,
Italian Classics you'll savour: Stuffed   Ltd.
Shells, Classic Lasagna, Manicotti
Florentine,Vegetable Lasagna, and
Classic Manicotti.
Hot Mamas' Large Spinach Tofu Ravioli☆   Hot Mamas'
Packed with tofu, spinach, carrots, onions,   Ravioli, Etc.
garlic, and spices.
SoyBoy® Ravioli❋☆   Northern Soy, Inc.
Made with organic tofu. Too
delicious for words.
SoyBoy Ravioli Verde™
Spinach pasta with garden herb filling.
SoyBoy Ravioli Rosa™
Tomato Pasta with roasted sweet

pepper filling.

The Soft Italian™☆ — R.F. Bakery International, Inc.
Soft filled breadsticks with tomato
sauce and real Italian taste! In
Mushroom or Vegetarian Beef
varieties.

Casalinga Tofu Ravioli☆ — Seenergy Foods Inc.
Filled with tofu and teeny-weeny
pieces of mixed vegetables.

Knishes

Legume® Potato Pockets — HKS Marketing, Ltd.
A knish by any other name would
still taste as great! Try Classic
Potato, Spinach, and Broccoli.

Klassic Knishes☆ — R.F. Bakery International, Inc.
You'll plotz once you try any
of these six fabulous flavors:
New York Style Potato,
Mediterranean Style Spice
Potato, Mushroom & Garlic,
Broccoli, Spinach, or Kasha.

Mexicana Olé!

Amy's Burritos — Amy's Kitchen Inc.
Breakfast Burrito, Bean &
Rice Burrito, and Black Bean
& Vegetable Burrito.

Black Bean & Vegetable Enchilada❀☆
Black Bean & Vegetable Enchilada Dinner❀☆
Complete dinner with Spanish Rice & Beans.

Mexican Tamale Pie
Cedarlane™ Low Fat Beans, Rice, Cedarlane Natural
& Cheese Style Burritoch   Foods, Inc.
Made with soy cheddar cheese.
Soypreme Tofu Enchilada Dinnerc
With Spanish brown rice and
refried beans.
Red Chile with Tofu Tamales☆   Col. Sanchez Traditional
These are very tasty tamales.   Foods Inc.
Soy Cheese & Vegetarian Bean Tostadac   Nature's
Completely gluten and yeast free.   Hilights, Inc.
Today's Tamales   Today's Traditions
Vegetable-Bean, Spicy Taco, and
Chick'n'Chile (all-vegetable).
Tumaro's™ Burritos   Tumaro's Homestyle
Three delicious varieties are   Kitchens
microwave-ready in just three
minutes. Black Bean, Non-
Dairy Cheesec, and Beans,
Rice & Potatoes.

Taste of the Orient

Green Guru™ International Cuisine   Deep Foods,
Flavorful Thai delights. Vegetable Pad   Inc.
Thai (tangy and spicy stir-fried rice
noodles with vegetables, tofu, spices
and ground peanuts) and Vegetable
Gaeng Daeng☆ (mixed vegetables
and tofu with basil, lime leaves,
red curry and coconut milk).
Lucky Pan-Fried Noodles   Lucky Food Co.
Lucky Spring Rolls☆

These are delectable, authentic
tasting little spring rolls.

Health is Wealth® Egg Rolls   Health is Wealth, Inc.
Hand-rolled with stone ground
whole wheat flour. Broccoli Tofu**c**,
Pizza Tofu**c**, and Spinach Tofu**c**
have delicious soy-cheesy taste.
Vegetarian☆ style is casein-free.

Sun's Veggie Light Oriental Dumplings☆   Sun Foods Ltd.
Scrumptious appetizers will remind you of
dinner at your favorite Chinese Restaurant.

Pizza

Soydance Pizza**c**❀   Amberwave Foods
Crispy organic whole wheat crust with
a tofu mozzarella cheese topping.

Roasted Vegetable Pizza**h**   Amy's Kitchen Inc.
Tasty cheeseless pizza with organic
shiitake mushrooms, artichokes, and
roasted bell peppers.

Cedarlane™ Garden Patch Pizza**ch**   Cedarlane Natural
Layered with colorful vegetables.   Foods, Inc.

Farm Foods Pizsoy Pizza**c**   The Hain Food
Made with an organic whole wheat crust.   Group, Inc.
Try Original, Fat-Free Cheese Style♥,
Fat-Free Garden Style♥, and Fat-Free
Vegetarian Pepperoni♥.

Rice Crust Soy Cheese Pizza**c**   Nature's Hilights, Inc.
Completely gluten and yeast free.

Special Delivery™ Organic Pizza**c**   Tree of Life, Inc.
Made with Soya Kaas™ soy cheese.

Pockets & Wraps

Pockets and wraps are tasty pastries stuffed with a variety of fillings. They are a delicious alternative to soup when you feel like a hot, quick, and satisfying lunch.

Vegetable Pot Pie Pocket**h**   Amy's Kitchen Inc.

Ken & Robert's Veggie Pockets   Imagine Foods, Inc.

10 delicious varieties baked in
wholesome organic wheat crust:
Greek**c**, Pizza**c**❀, Oriental, Tex-
Mex**c**, Indian☆, Potato and
Cheddar**c**, Pot Pie, Santa Fe**c**,
Broccoli and Cheddar**c**, and
Bar-B-Que☆.

Cedarlane™ Low Fat Teriyaki   Cedarlane Natural Foods,

Veggie Wrap**h**   Inc.

Key to Symbols

❤ Fat Free
☆ Author's Favorite
❀ Kid's Pick
c Contains casein or caseinate
h Contains honey

8

Fun Foods for Parties, Holidays, and Special Occasions

· ·

...Earth is generous
With her provision, and her sustenance
Is very kind; she offers, for your table,
Food that requires no bloodshed and no slaughter.
- Ovid

The entries featured in this chapter are truly worth celebrating. Delight your family on holidays (or any day) with a healthful and delicious tofu turkey. Impress your party guests with elegant hors d'oeuvres, pâtés, and smoked tofu sensations. And when you want to savour the taste of down-home goodness while letting someone else do the cooking, try any of the homemade edibles recommended here. With the help of the foods in this chapter, you'll be able to turn any meal into a delectably elegant, ambrosial affair.

Thanksgiving Feast

Tofurky™
A prebaked, vegetarian stuffed
tofu roast turkey with dark
tempeh drumettes and golden
gravy. Available by special
order through health food
stores or by calling Turtle
Island. Serves 8.

Turtle Island Foods, Inc.

....
QUICK TIP: THANKSGIVING TO REMEMBER
Except for the bird, the Thanksgivings you've always enjoyed
have been predominantly vegetarian affairs. Along with a
stuffed tofu turkey, serve a large tossed salad, cranberry
sauce, sweet potatoes, gravy, and green beans to begin a
tradition of truly memorable, delicious, healthful, and
compassionate holiday celebrations.
....

Pâté

D'Artagnan Vegetable Terrine ☆
Whether you're planning an elegant
dinner party, want to entice your
friends, or just treat yourself to
something truly special, enjoy this
scrumptious, gorgeous terrine. It's
three colorful layers of wild mushrooms,
roasted red bell pepper, and spinach will
please even the most refined palate.
This rich pâté is available in upscale

D'Artagnan, Inc.

gourmet food specialty shops or you
can order direct from D'Artagnan.
Warning: this product is addictive
and expensive, (but worth it!)

Bonavita Vegetarian Pâté   Liberty Richter Inc.
Imported from Switzerland
in Garlic and Herb varieties.

Madame Sophie's Vegetable Pâté   Quong Hop & Co.
by Spa Cuisine☆
Sensational taste--spread on baguette,
crackers, pita, or bagels. Low fat and
totally organic.

Hearty Life™ Gourmet European Spread   Sovex Foods, Inc.
Low-fat vegetable pâtés: Garlic, Mushroom,
Herb, Green Peppercorn, and Traditional.

Smoked Tofu

Sliced thinly, and placed on a cracker, smoked tofu is
reminiscent of the taste of smoked gouda cheese.

Tree of Life® Smoked Tofu   Tree of Life, Inc.
Organically grown soybeans and
a fabulous, true smoked flavor in
Original and Hot 'N Spicy☆.

Organic Smoked Tofu[h]   Wildwood Natural Foods
Long hours of marination and
basking in Wildwood's smoke
house, give this tofu a superbly
creamy texture and rich mellow
flavor. In Mild Szechuan☆ or
Garlic Teriyaki flavors.

Hors d'oeuvres

Health is Wealth® Munchees   Health is Wealth Inc.
These bite-size taste treats are
like miniature egg rolls. Pizza**c**,
Broccoli**c**, Spinach**c**, and Mexican**c**,
styles are made with soy cheese.
Veggie☆ style is casein-free.

Homemade Delights

Gourmet Tamales™☆   Gourmet Tamales
Like no tamales you've ever
tasted. Shipped to you frozen
and ready to eat in less than five
minutes in your microwave.
Tomatillo Salsa, Chipotle Salsa,
Spicy Potato in Banana Leaf,
Spicy Mushroom-Garlic, Green
Mole & Vegetables, Corn, Scallion,
& Jalapeno, Red Mole-Green Beans,
and Potato-Cilantro. Dessert tamales
(yum!) in: Pineapple-Raisin and
Strawberry-Apple flavors.
Kisses Knishes**h**☆   Knishworks
Although made in a commercial
bakery, these wonderful knishes
are so reminiscent of the old-style
New York knishes I remember
devouring with glee as a kid, they
deserve to be labeled "made with
homemade goodness." The tofu
varieties are as scrumptious as any

cheese knish I've ever tasted. Tofu
Apple Raisin, Tofu Pineapple, Tofu
Blueberry, Tofu Spinach, Tofu
Broccoli, Potato, Potato Spinach,
Potato Broccoli, Potato Mixed
Vegetable, Kasha, Chili, Brown Rice
& Broccoli, Brown Rice & Vegetable,
and Brown Rice & Spinach.

Organic Gourmet Creations☆   Marscell The Organic
Imagine freshly prepared entrees,   Gourmet
pies, and pastries lovingly made in
small batches by an experienced,
nutritionally enlightened chef. The
selections change as Marscell uses
only items in season, so call for the
current menu. Not available in stores
anywhere, but when you're ready to
savour the sweetest sensations, tastiest
ethnic dishes, and most scrumptious
special occasion pastries, Marscell will
be happy to ship them directly to your
front doorstep. Following is a partial
list of rotating menu selections. Always
request that your dishes be made vegan.
Entrees: Burritos, Enchiladas, Calzone,
Savory Hunza Pie, Indian Rice, Five
Vegetable Pie, Lasagna, Tamale Pie, Pizza,
Potato Pie, Shepherd's Pie and Veggie
Burgers. Fresh baked goods: Apricot,
Apple, Berry, and Peach Pies, Whole
Wheat Citrus Cake, and Raspberry filled
or Carob Brownies. Special Occasion
Vegan Pastries (all beautifully gift wrapped):

Valentine Chocolate Cake, Valentine Brownies,
Mother's Day Carrot Cake, Father's Day Rum
Soaked Crunchy Cookies or Chocolate Chip
Cookies, Thanksgiving Biscotti in Pistachio
or Pine Nut (plain or chocolate dipped!), and
Christmas Gourmet Whole Wheat Fruit Cake.

Key to Symbols

❤ Fat Free
☆ Author's Favorite
❀ Kid's Pick
c Contains casein or caseinate
h Contains honey

9

Desserts: Ice Dreams and Beyond

. . . .

Nothing will benefit human health and increase chances for survival on
Earth as much as the evolution to a vegetarian diet.
- Albert Einstein

Sorbet

I have not tasted ice cream in years and I no longer miss
it. Why? Because I fell in love with sorbet! It's delectably
smooth, fruity, satisfying, and fat-free! (Chocolate flavored
sorbets contain a negligible amount of fat from the cocoa
powder). You can enjoy the creamy, rich taste of sorbet
without the guilt, bloat, and mucous-forming side effects of
dairy frozen desserts. Most sorbet is completely free of
animal products, but make sure you check the label for egg
white. Some companies add it to their chocolate flavored
sorbet. Of course, the sorbets featured here do not contain
any egg white.

....

Ben & Jerry's Sorbet♥   Ben & Jerry's
Satisfying and delicious with   Homemade, Inc.
bits of real fruit: Mocha, Piña
Colada, Purple Passion Fruit,
Pink Lemonade☆, Strawberry
Kiwi, and Doonesberry.
Sorbet Pops♥❀
Doonesberry and
Strawberry Kiwi.
Cascadian Farm® Organic Sorbet♥   Cascadian Farm
Raspberry, Strawberry, Blackberry,
Peach, Chocolate, Banana Bliss,
Mango Magic, Luscious Lemon, and
Guava Passion.
Cascadian Farm Organic Sorbet Bars♥❀
Chocolate, Mango, Strawberry,
Orange, and Raspberry.
Double Rainbow® Sorbet♥   Double Rainbow
Silky smooth and creamy.   Gourmet Ice Creams, Inc.
Chocolate☆❀, Kiwi, Marion
Blackberry☆, Orange, and
Raspberry❀.
Dreyer's Whole Fruit™ Sorbet♥   Dreyer's Grand
Strawberry☆, Raspberry,   Ice Cream
Lemon, and Peach.
Real Fruit™ Chunky Sorbet♥☆   Eskimo Pie
Made with real fruit chunks!   Corporation
Red Raspberry, Lemon Peel,
Georgia Peach, Mountain
Strawberry, Tropical Blend,
Wild Berries❀, Ruby Red
Grapefruit, Strawberry-Banana❀,
Cranberry-Raspberry, and

Watermelon-Strawberry.

<u>Pascal's™ Premium French Sorbet</u>♥☆   Glacier Gourmet,
All natural , silky smooth , sensuous   Inc.
taste. Strawberry, Lime, Passion Fruit,
Raspberry, Lemon, Orange, Mango,
Chocolate❀, and Peach.

<u>Howler Rainforest Fruit Sorbet</u>♥☆   Howler Products
Delicious, creamy adventures for your
mouth! Made from rare forest fruits,
the purchase of which supports rain
forest preservation projects. Guava
Strawberry, Passion Fruit, Mango,
Primal Scream Coffee Bean! (a delicious
way to stay awake), Caribbean Cherry,
Guanabana, Dark Forest Chocolate,
Tropical Tangerine, Mayan Blackberry,
and Rainforest Raspberry.

<u>Columbo Sorbet</u>♥   Integrated Brands
Wildberry☆, Peach, Mango,   Inc.
Lemon, Strawberry, and Raspberry.

<u>Columbo Sorbet Pops</u>♥
Wildberry.❀☆

<u>Tofutti® Sorbet</u>♥   Tofutti Brands, Inc.
Chocolate, Strawberry, Orange
Peach Mango, Lemon, Coffee,
and Raspberry Tea.

Dairy-Free Ice Dreams

Many of these desserts closely resemble the ice creams
they imitate in both taste and texture. They are great in
sundaes, floats, or drizzled with syrup. For an outrageously
decadent change of pace, try topping any of these frozen

treats with the dessert salsas listed on page 90. Best of all,
you can joyfully serve these desserts to your delighted
children because you will know that they are completely free
of animal based ingredients.

Rice Dream® Non Dairy Dessert   Imagine Foods, Inc.
Cappuccino, Carob, Carob Almond,
Cherry Vanilla, Chocolate, Chocolate
Chip, Cocoa Marble Fudge, Mint Carob
Chip, Orange Vanilla Swirl❀☆ (tastes
just like a creamsicle!), Strawberry,
Vanilla, and Vanilla Swiss Almond.
Rice Dream® Supreme
Great new flavor sensations: Cappuccino
Almond Fudge, Cherry Chocolate Chunk☆,
Chocolate Almond Chunk, Chocolate
Fudge Brownie☆, Double Espresso Bean,
Mint Chocolate Cookie☆, Peanut Butter
Cup❀, and Pralines N' Dream.
Rice Dream® Pies❀☆
Two oatmeal cookies with a malt
sweetened carob or chocolate coating.
Vanilla Dream Pie w/Carob
Mocha Dream Pie w/Carob
Chocolate Dream Pie w/Chocolate
Mint Dream Pie w/Chocolate.
Rice Dream® Bars❀
Rice Dream dipped in malt
sweetened chocolate or carob.
Vanilla w/Carob, Strawberry
w/Carob, and Chocolate
w/Chocolate.
Rice Dream® Nutty Bars❀

Rice Dream dipped in malt
sweetened chocolate and
covered with peanuts.
Vanilla or Chocolate.

Rice Dream® Cones**h**❀
Crunchy, chocolate lined
cones filled with Vanilla
or Chocolate and topped with
peanuts and rich chocolate.

Tofutti® Lowfat Non Dairy Frozen Dessert   Toffuti
Creamy 98% fat-free dessert sold in pints: Brands, Inc.
Vanilla Fudge, Chocolate Fudge, Coffee
Marshmallow Swirl, Strawberry Banana,
Passion Island Fruit, and Peach Mango.

Tofutti Frutti™❤
Non-dairy, fat-free, sweetened only
with fruit juice, and containing non-
dairy acidophilus cultures. Three
Berry, Apricot Mango, and
Vanilla Apple Orchard.

Tofutti Frutti™ Chocolate Dipped Pops❀
Vanilla cream with Tutti-Frutti sorbet.

Tofutti® Teddy Fudge Pops❀
The great taste of a real fudge bar!

Tofutti® Chocolate Fudge Treats❤
Fat-free and sugar free with real
fudge taste!

It's Soy Delicious™   Turtle Mountain,
Fruit sweetened creamy dessert   Inc.
in pints: Espresso, Awesome
Chocolate❀, Vanilla Fudge,
Vanilla, Raspberry, Chocolate
Peanut Butter❀, Espresso Almond

Fudge, and Carob Peppermint.

<u>Sweet Nothings™ Frozen Dessert</u>♥
Creamy and fruity flavors in pints:
Black Leopard, Chocolate❀,
Chocolate Mandarin☆, Tiger Stripes,
Vanilla, Espresso Fudge, Very
Berry Blueberry, Raspberry Swirl,
Mango Raspberry☆, Passion Island,
and Piña Colada.

<u>Sweet Nothings Sundae Bars</u>
Chocolate covered dessert bars:
Espresso Almond Fudge, Chocolate
Peanut Butter❀, Chocolate, and
Vanilla Crunch❀.

<u>Sweet Nothings Fat-Free Bars</u>♥
Fudge, Mocha Mania, Passion
Island, and Mango Raspberry.

Dessert Toppings

<u>Hawaiian Kukui® Fruit Syrups</u>
These tropical fruit syrups are
simply sensational. Pour them
over frozen desserts. They also
make delicious toppings for
pancakes and waffles! Guava,
Coconut☆, Passion Fruit,
Pineapple, Mango, Papaya,
and Macadamia Nut.

Hawaiian Fruit
Specialties Ltd.

<u>Fat-Free Chocolate Ecstasy</u>™♥
Decadently rich tasting, dark
chocolate topping. Incredibly
smooth and delicious.

Newmarket Foods,
Inc.

<u>Southwest Spirit™ Seductive Dessert Salsas</u>   RGE, Inc.
Drizzle these toppings over frozen "ice dreams"
or cakes and indulge yourself in dessert heaven.
Made from sweet fruits, brandy, and a hint
of chile. They turn ordinary desserts into a
lusciously exotic taste experience. Brandied
Cherries Diablo, Brandied Apricots Diablo,
and Brandied Chocolate Raspberries Diablo☆.

Brownies

<u>Vegan Decadence Brownies</u>   Frankly Natural
They're as devilishly delicious   Bakers
as the name implies. Mocha,
Chocolate❀☆, and Carob.

Pies

<u>Natural Feast™ Gourmet Streusel Pies</u>☆   Natural Feast
Fabulous fruity fillings, and scrumptious   Corp.
pie crusts made without hydrogenated oils.
Packed frozen and unbaked, just heat in
your oven. No one will believe you didn't
bake them from scratch. Natural Apple,
Cherry, and Blueberry.

Chocolate Candies

You won't find any wimpy milk chocolates here. Just
rich, deep, dark chocolate sensations. Chocaholics beware!
The following listings are highly habit-forming.

<u>Tropical Source® Organic Chocolate Bars</u>   Cloud Nine, Inc.

Dairy-free and delicious in ten innovative
flavors: Sundried Jungle Banana☆, Java
Roast, Hazlenut Espresso Crunch, Green
Tea Crisp, Wild Rice Crisp❀, California
Raisins & Currants❀☆, Mint Candy Crunch,
Red Raspberry Crush❀☆, Maple Almond
Granola, and Toasted Almond.

Sweet River Chocolates™   Community
Distinctively smooth texture in   Products, Inc.
four delectable flavors: Chocolate,
Raspberry☆, Rainforest Crunch®,
and Dark Chocolate & Espresso.

Dolphin Natural Chocolates™   Dolphin Natural
Hand made and malt sweetened   Chocolates
individual chocolate delights
wrapped in pretty foil paper.
A portion of profits benefit
environmental organizations.
Mint Crisp☆, Almond Toffee**h**,
Organic Peanut Butter❀, Solid
Dark Chocolate, Roasted Almond,
Espresso Nut, and Cashew Coconut
Raisin☆.

Ghirardelli Dark Chocolate with   Ghirardelli
Raspberries☆   Chocolate Company
As enticing as it sounds!

Rapunzel™ Organic Swiss Chocolate Bars   Mercantile
Three great flavors sweetened with   Food Company
Rapadura™ (unrefined, evaporated
sugar cane juice) and boasting a
distinctly adult taste: Bittersweet
Chocolate, Bittersweet Chocolate with
Almonds, and Bittersweet Chocolate

with Hazelnuts.

Newman's Own™ Organics Chocolate Bars   Newman's
Sweet Dark Chocolate Bars in Plain,   Own Organics
Espresso, and Orange flavors.

Sunspire® Natural Chocolate Earth Balls   Sunspire
Make everyday Earth Day with these foil-
wrapped chocolate sweeties.

Cookies

Barbara's® Bakery Homestyle Cookies♥   Barbara's
Moist, chewy, and fruit juice sweetened.   Bakery, Inc.
Chocolate Mint, Oatmeal Raisin, Chewy
Chocolate, and Nutt'n Crispies.
Barbara's Bakery Fat Free Fig Bars♥☆
Whole Wheat, Wheat Free, or Raspberry❀.
Snackimals™ Animal Cookies❀
Chocolate Chip, Vanilla, and
Oatmeal-Wheat Free.

Love Dreams Coconut Cookies❀☆   Food For Living
Wheat-free, chewy, moist, and delicious
fluffy coconut macaroon sensations.
Original, Double Chocolate, Vanilla
Rainbow, and Chocolate Rainbow.

Frankly Natural Cookies & Squares   Frankly Natural
Dairy-free, wheat-free, and tasty   Bakers
energy snacks or dessert treats.
Made with tahini, sesame, and
sunflower seeds. Cookies: Rice,
Coconut❀☆, Apricot-Almond,
Raisin❀ and Rainforest. Squares:
Currant, Pecan, Carob, Cashew-
Apricot, and Date-Nut.

Original Oat Bran Graham Crackers**h**   Health Valley
Yay! Graham crackers without   Foods, Inc.
hydrogenated oils!
Heaven Scent 96% Fat Free Cookies   Heaven Scent
Fruit juice sweetened and wheat free.   Natural Foods Co.
Chocolate Fudge, Carob Fudge, Apple
N' Spice, Mountain Berry, and Old
Fashion Raisin.
PretzelCookie™❀   J&J Snack Foods
It's a pretzel! It's a cookie! No, it's   Corp.
a tasty twist in cookies. Lemon,
Ginger, Vanilla, Oatmeal, or
Chocolate.
Jacqui's Gourmet Cookies❀☆   Jacqui's Gourmet
Scandalously moist, chewy, and   Cookies, Etc.
delicious! Chocolate Chip, Fudge
Brownie, Cinnamon Raisin, and
Lemon Sesame.
Nana's Cookies☆   Nana's Cookie
The original "feel good cookie"   Company
is sweetened with real maple
syrup. A high carbohydrate
energy food that tastes great.
Macrobiotic, low calorie, and
low fat in three flavors: Oatmeal
Chocolate Chip, Oatmeal Raisin,
and Oatmeal Sunflower.
Natural Ovens Cookies   Natural Ovens of
Great tasting cookies with all   Manitowoc Wisconsin
natural ingredients that are
good for you, too. Made with
oats, sunflower seeds, wheat
germ, and flax. Oatmeal Raisin

and Chip Mate (carob chips and
coconut).

Sistah's® Cookies**h**   Orean's Express, Inc.
Chocolate Carob Chip and
Oatmeal Raisin☆.

Small World™ Animal Grahams✵☆   Tree of Life, Inc.
Graham cracker cookies made
without hydrogenated oils are
fashioned in the shapes of
endangered species. For kids
and adults alike. Plain and
Chocolate Chip varieties.

Cookie Lovers™ Creme Supremes✵☆
The first all natural chocolate
sandwich cookie to taste like an
Oreo. Also in Mint and Royal
Vanilla flavors.

Fat-Free Cookies**h**❤
Golden Oatmeal Raisin and
Harvest Fruit & Nut.

Honey-Sweet Cookies**h**
Oh-So-Oatmeal.

Soft-Cookies
Maui Macaroon☆, Double Trouble
Fudge, Old-Fashioned Oatmeal,
and Positively Peanut Butter.

Donuts

The One and Only Eggless Doughnut   Vegetarian Health,
This rich, high-fat doughnut tastes   Inc.
sinfully scrumptious! Note: Carob
Coated variety is the one and only

flavor that does not contain any
hydrogenated oil.

Pudding

Instant Rice Pudding   Dr. McDougall's Right
Tasty pudding in a cup   Foods, Inc.
with vanilla and cinnamon.
Just add boiling water!
Amazake Pudding   Grainaissance Inc.
Naturally sweet and tasty.
Almond, Chocolate☆, and
Lemon❤.
Imagine Pudding Snacks☆   Imagine Foods, Inc.
Chocolate❀, Banana❀, Lemon,
and Butterscotch.
Mori-Nu Mates Pudding & Pie Mix**h**   Morinaga
Simply blend with Mori-Nu lite tofu   Nutritional Foods,
in your blender or food processor   Inc.
for a sensationally rich and creamy
dessert. Note: These mixes contain
a very small amount of coconut oil.
Lemon Creme❀, Chocolate☆❀,
and Cappuccino.

QUICK TIP: DAIRY FREE TOFU WHIPPED CREAM
Combine 1 lb. soft tofu, 1 Tbsp. vanilla extract, 1 tsp.
almond extract, 1/4 cup sugar, and 1/8 cup soy milk in a
food processor or blender. Refrigerate before serving, then
dollop over brownies, pudding, or fruit flavored gelatin!

Fruit Gelatin

Surprisingly few people really know what gelatin is made of. I'll never forget the time I was invited to a friend's home for Christmas dinner. There, sitting on the table at each place setting, was a compact little blob of opaque green goo, shaking and shimmying atop a curled lettuce leaf. When I politely declined to eat it, the hostess was clearly insulted and exclaimed, "But I made this especially for you!"

Not wishing to dampen the joy of the season any further, I elected not to tell the hostess that animal bones, cartilage, tendons, hooves and other slaughterhouse byproducts were used in making the shiny, green globules. I simply didn't eat the one placed before me.

Emes Kosher-Jel®♥✿☆   Emes Kosher Products
Taste just like the fruity gelatins
you loved as a kid, only they're
better because they're completely
vegetarian. Sweetened with sucrose
or fructose in eleven fun and fruity
flavors: Cherry, Raspberry, Lemon,
Strawberry, Lime, Orange, Grape,
Pineapple, Mandarin Orange, Black
Cherry, and Black Raspberry.

Organic Fruit Gel Snack♥✿   Made In Nature
A sweet ready-made treat that tastes
like flavored gelatin without animal
ingredients! Apple, Lemon, Orange,
and Strawberry.

Key to Symbols: ♥ Fat Free ☆Author's Favorite ✿ Kid's Pick
c Contains casein or caseinate **h** Contains honey

10

Coffee Substitutes: Kicking Caffeine

. . . .

What is this demilitarized zone? Whatever it is, I like it! Gets you on
your toes better than a strong cup of cappuccino!
- Robin Williams in Good Morning Vietnam

Have you been thinking about kicking the caffeine habit?
Many people who eliminate meat from their diets find that they
can no longer tolerate the "caffeine jitters."

There are also a number of health conditions for which
doctors advise their patients to eliminate coffee. It is believed
that caffeine may contribute to such problems as acid
indigestion, anxiety, irritability and nervousness, fibrocystic
breast disease, migraines or other vascular headaches,
insomnia, and kidney or bladder problems. Caffeine also
depletes the body of calcium. Therefore, if you are concerned
about osteoporosis, it is advisable to limit your caffeine intake.

Following are delicious, naturally caffeine-free beverages
that are rich enough to lure even the most confirmed coffee
drinker.

....

Coffee Substitutes

Inka♥☆

From Poland, a rich, natural instant
grain beverage made from roasted
rye, barley, beets and chicory roots.

Adambra Imports,
Inc.

Pero®♥

Instant natural grain beverage
from Germany. Made from barley,
malted barley, chicory, and rye.

Alpursa

Bambu®♥

Swiss instant grain beverage
made with chicory, figs,
wheat, malted barley and
roasted acorns.

Bioforce of
America, Ltd.

Cafix®♥

Imported from Germany,
this fine instant grain beverage
is made from malt, chicory,
barley, rye, figs and beet
roots.

Cafix of North America,
Inc.

Dacopa™ Roasted Dahlia Powder♥

A unique, full-bodied instant beverage
made from the root of the dahlia flower.
You'll notice a hint of sweetness from
fructose which occurs naturally in the
dahlia tuber. Dissolve in cold or hot
water, or prepare with hot soy milk
to make a tasty mocha-like drink
that both kids and adults can enjoy.

California Natural
Products

Yannoh♥

A satisfying Swiss grain beverage

Eden Foods, Inc.

made with organic barley, organic
rye, organic malted barley,
chicory, and acorns.

QUICK TIP: KISS CAFFEINE GOODBYE
When preparing your coffee drink, start with equal parts of
coffee and instant grain beverage. Gradually reduce the
amount of coffee and increase the amount of grain beverage
each day. Soon you will find that you are enjoying a
completely caffeine-free, flavorful alternative to coffee
without the unpleasant side effects of caffeine withdrawal.

Postum® Instant Hot Beverage♥   Kraft General Foods,
The original grain beverage   Inc.
introduced by C.W. Post over
a century ago is still a popular
favorite after all these years.
Made from wheat bran, wheat
molasses, and maltodextrin
(from corn). In Regular and
Natural Coffee Flavor.

Instant! Sipp Natural Coffee Substitute♥   Modern Products,
Imported from Italy and made with 100%   Inc.
certified organic ingredients: roasted barley,
chicory, rye, chick pea, and fig.

Sundance Barley Brew♥   Sundance Roasting
This savory organic alternative   Company, Inc.
is brewed just like coffee--drip,
perk, or espresso. Made from
100% organically grown barley.

....

Teeccino™ Caffeine-Free Herbal Coffee♥☆   Teeccino
Now you can make scrumptious caffeine   Caffé, Inc.
free cappuccinos and lattes with this
enticing herbal coffee made from carob,
barley, chicory root, Persian figs, dates
and almonds. Teeccino is brewable, and
boasts a rich, full-bodied flavor. Delicious
hot or cold. The fragrant aroma is enticing.
In Original, Almond Amaretto, Chocolate
Mint, Vanilla Nut, Hazelnut, Java, and
Mocha flavors.

Natural Touch® Kaffree™ Roma♥   Worthington
Rich tasting instant roasted grain   Foods, Inc.
grain beverage made from roasted
barley malt, roasted barley, and
roasted chicory.

Hot Chocolate

Ghirardelli Hot Chocolates   Ghirardelli Chocolate
Vegan hot cocoa mixes from heaven!   Company
Mix with soy milk for a rich, creamy
cocoa. Try Double Chocolate❊, Pralines
& Cream♥☆, or Chocolate Hazelnut☆.

Tea

There is an enormous array of wonderful tasting, herbal, naturally caffeine-free tea available. However, most herbal teas would not satisfy a coffee drinker's craving for a rich, full-bodied beverage. The following teas are exceptionally rich and so amazingly satisfying that they live up to the challenge.

Raja's Cup™❤✩
Brews like coffee, tastes like
coffee, and it's good for you.
Loaded with antioxidents (that
are reportedly 100's of times
more powerful than vitamin C
or E). Made from rare and
delicious Ayurvedic herbs for
a rich-roasted flavor and it's
100% naturally caffeine free.

Maharishi Ayur-Ved
Products International,
Inc.

Yogi Tea™❤
These savory and exotic blends are
available in tea bags to enjoy as quick,
satisfying beverages, or by the pound
for cappuccino, latte, or brewed iced
spice tea. Tahitian Vanilla✩, Carob
Mint, Egyptian Licorice, Cinnamon
Spice, Hazelnut Cream✩, Mango
Passion, and Maple Royale✩.

The Yogi Tea
Company

Key to Symbols

❤ Fat Free
✩ Author's Favorite
✻ Kid's Pick
c Contains casein or caseinate
h Contains honey

11

The Pet Department: Fluffy and Fido Go Veggie!

· ·

I care not for a man's religion whose dog
and cat are not the better for it.
- Abraham Lincoln

The ugly truth about commercial pet foods is that in addition to the high levels of toxic pesticides, chemical additives, and hormones which make up your pet's meat-based diet, you can add slaughterhouse waste and road kill to the menu. Many of the diseases which threaten the health of our pets may be directly related to their diets.

Dogs are omnivores and easily adapt to an all vegetarian diet. Cats, on the other hand, are true carnivores and require special nutrients found in a meat based diet. Taurine, an essential amino acid, is manufactured in the bodies of all mammals except cats. They lack the ability to produce taurine and so they must get it from their diet, or succumb to blindness, disease, and death. Fortunately, modern technology has helped researchers to develop a process for extracting taurine from sea-vegetables. The all vegetarian cat foods listed here are supplemented with all the nutrients (taurine and essential fatty acids) felines require for optimum health and well-being.

Both of my companion animals are life-long vegetarians. In fact, they are vegans, consuming no dairy or eggs. My cat, Indiana Jones, and my dog, Cicely Alaska have enjoyed the best of health, beauty, and vigor. Your pets can thrive on a completely vegetarian diet too, with the help of the following plant-based pet food products.

Canned Dog Food

Evolution Diet™ Peas & Avocado for Dogs   Evolution Pet
Uses only the most wholesome and natural   Foods
ingredients for your pet.
Vegetarian Dog Formula   Natural Life Pet
Endorsed by Cicely Alaska.   Products, Inc.
Vegetarian Canine Formula   Nature's Recipe Pet Foods
PetGuard® Premium Vegetarian Feast Dinner   PetGuard, Inc.

Kibble for Dogs

Evolution Diet Pasta Seafood   Evolution Pet Foods
Vegetarian Dog Formula   Natural Life Pet Products, Inc.
Vegetarian Canine Formula   Nature's Recipe Pet Foods

Dog Biscuits and Treats

Bark Bars®   American Health Kennels
Adorable healthy treats shaped
like mailmen and cats. Garlic, Peanut
Butter, and Wheat & Corn Free.

Willie & Tess' Boss of the House Bars   Boss Bars
Made from 100% organic ingredients in
Original and Wheat & Corn Free varieties.
Dandy Doggie Gourr-met Dog Treats   Dandy Doggie
Gourr-geous gourr-met gifts for your
favorite canine companion. This collection
is made exclusively from organic whole
wheat flour and other all natural ingredients.
The treats are beautifully packaged and
adorned with raffia, purple, and gold ribbons.
Bowownies™ - Carob flavored brownie squares.
Bowownies™ with Nuts
Bowser Brittle™ - Rainforest nut treat.
Bone-Anza™ - A VERY BIG bone.
New Chow Mein - Noodle shaped treats.
Biscotti per Bowser - A dozen assorted dog biscuits.
The Canine Baker Granpaws® Natural Dog Treats   Doca
In four varieties: USA, Inc.
Granpaws Pooch Pleasers made with peanut butter,
Granpaws Granola Bone with garlic,
Granpaws Doggie Cookies made with oat bran, and
Granpaws Mini Bites made with oat bran.
Healthy Cookies for T.V. Watching Dogs   Healthy Pet
Formulated for weight-conscious canines,   Products
these tasty treats are available in fat-free or low
fat all vegetarian varieties. Wheat-free, Garlic,
Chicken, and Beef flavors. Note: Specify non-
glazed when ordering. (Glaze contains egg whites).
Nature's Animals® All Natural Dog Biscuits   Nature's
Handmade treats preserved with vitamin E.   Animals, Inc.
Apple Ring, Peanut Butter, and Vegetarian.
Mrs. Poochee's® Gourmet Cookies for Dogs   Orean's
These big, beautiful cookies look so tasty   Express, Inc.

you'll be tempted to eat them yourself.
Stop that! They're for your pooch.

Mr. Barky's™ Vegetarian Dog Biscuits   PetGuard, Inc.
Purr-Fect Growlings® Dog Biscuit Treats   Purr-Fect
Simple ingredients in great tasting treats   Growlings
that are baked in the shape of the state
of California and also in hearts.

Hempy Dog™ Hempseed Dog Treats   Vermont Hemp
Hemp provides 21 amino acids, 14   Company
essential fatty acids, 32 trace minerals,
antioxidents, B vitamins, and is a
complete high-quality source of non-
animal protein.

Pet Pastries, Gourmet Cookies   Wow Bow Distributors
Beautiful, healthy, gourmet line   Ltd.
of freshly baked treats like bagels,
snowballs, mini-croissants, and
even birthday cakes. All vegetarian,
many completely vegan. Call to
receive their free catalogue.

Canned Cat Food

Evolution Diet Peas & Avocado for Cats   Evolution Pet
Only the finest ingredients for your cat.   Foods

Kibble for Cats

Evolution Diet Pasta Seafood
Completely vegetarian with added taurine.

Canine/Feline Kibble

Anergen III™   Wysong Corporation

Contains taurine and essential
fatty acids for cats. Complete
nutrition for dogs, too.

Feline Dietary Supplement

Vegecat™   Harbingers of a New Age
Because cats are true carnivores,
they need certain nutrients like
taurine, that formerly only flesh
foods could provide. If cats don't
get enough of this secondary amino
acid (which other mammals convert
from the essential amino acids methionine
and cystine), they may become blind or
suffer from serious heart disease. Just
add Vegecat to one of the simple to prepare,
veterinarian approved recipes provided,
and your cat can safely enjoy a completely
cruelty-free diet.

Canine Dietary Supplement

Vegedog™
Dogs are nutritional omnivores
so they do not have the same
metabolic limitations as cats.
But achieving the proper nutrient
balance in their diets isn't always
easy if you want to stay away from
commercially prepared dog foods and
feed whole, fresh foods from your kitchen.
Vegedog eliminates any guesswork.

When used with the recipes provided,
you can be assured of meeting the
dietary recommendations for dogs.

Dog Chews

Booda Velvets™

Made from a revolutionary
new corn starch formula.
Completely free of animal
by-products, preservatives,
and toxins. In several sizes
and flavors: Premium Mix,
Chicken, and Beef & Vegetable.

Aspen Pet Products, Inc.

Appendix I

Networking Resources

Write or call the following organizations for information on vegetarianism and related subjects:

American Natural Hygiene Society
12816 Race Track Road
Tampa, FL 33625
813-855-6607

American Vegan Society
Box H
Malaga, NJ 08328
609-694-2887

EarthSave International
706 Frederick Street
Santa Cruz, CA 95062-2205
408-423-4069

Eating with Conscience Campaign
Humane Society of the United States
700 Professional Drive
Gaithersburg, MD 20879
301-258-3054

Farm Animal Reform Movement (FARM)
Box 30654
Bethesda, MD 20824
301-530-5747

Farm Sanctuary East
P.O. Box 150
Watkins Glen, NY 14891
607-583-2225

Farm Sanctuary West
P.O. Box 1065
Orland, CA 95963
916-865-4617

Friends Vegetarian Society of North America (Quaker)
P.O. Box 53354
Washington, DC 20009

Jewish Vegetarians of North America
6938 Reliance Road
Federalsburg, MD 21632
410-754-5550

North American Vegetarian Society
P.O. Box 72
Dolgeville, NY 13329
518-568-7970

People for the Ethical Treatment of Animals (PETA)
501 Front Street
Norfolk, VA 23570
757-622-1078

Physicians Committee for Responsible Medicine (PCRM)
5100 Wisconsin Ave. - Suite 404
Washington, DC 20016
202-686-2210

United Poultry Concerns
P.O. Box 59367
Potomac, MD 20859
301-948-2406

Vegan Action
P.O. Box 4353
Berkeley, CA 94704
510-654-6297

Vegetarian Awareness Network
P.O. Box 321
Knoxville, TN 37901
800-EAT-VEGE

Vegetarian Resource Group
P.O. Box 1463
Baltimore, MD 21203
410-366-VEGE

Vegetarian Union of North America (VUNA)
P.O. Box 9710
Washington, DC 20016
617-625-3790

Voice for a Viable Future
11288 Ventura Blvd. #202A
Studio City, CA 91604
818-509-1255

Appendix II

Vegetarian Resources on the Internet

The following websites provide valuable information on a variety of topics of interest to vegetarians. You can get answers to health questions, download the latest news articles and recipes, find out about exciting vegetarian events, become informed about animal rights issues, learn about the environmental impact of your food choices, and even chat with other vegetarians. Many of these sites will link you to other websites. Once you begin exploring the web, you'll discover many more resources on your own.

Animal Rights Resource Site
http://www.envirolink.org/arrs/
A comprehensive and well-organized source of information about all aspects of animal rights, including a platform for free and open discussion.

EarthSave International
http://www.earthsave.org/
EarthSave International is a non-profit global movement which promotes the benefits of plant-based foods for personal health, a sustainable environment, and a more compassionate world.

Farm Animal Reform Movement (FARM)
http://www.envirolink.org/arrs/farm/
Farm Animal Reform Movement campaigns for the rights of farmed animals, promotes wholesome plant-based eating, and encourages environmental consciousness. Visit this site to learn about FARM's five national programs, including the Great American Meatout.

Farm Sanctuary
http://www.farmsanctuary.org/
Farm Sanctuary is dedicated to stopping the exploitation of

animals used for food production. Since its inception in 1986, Farm Sanctuary has devoted its resources and time to exposing and ending the cruel practices of the "food animal" industry. This website provides a wide range of information on campaigns to fight animal abuses, news articles, and vegetarianism.

New Veg
http://www.newveg.av.org/
Not just for the new or wanna-be vegetarian, NewVeg is a non-profit organization dedicated to smashing myths and delivering the truth regarding human nutrition. This site is for people interested in learning more about a cholesterol-free (vegan) diet with an emphasis on raw foods. NewVeg is also a great entertainment value for all the many dedicated veggie veterans out there in cyberland.

North American Vegetarian Society (NAVS)
http://www.cyberveg.org/navs/
NAVS is a nonprofit educational organization dedicated to promoting vegetarianism. At this website you can get info about and register to attend Summerfest, an annual conference presented by the North American Vegetarian Society for the past 23 years. At Summerfest you can learn from experts in the fields of health, nutrition, exercise, animal rights and the environment. It's a wonderful opportunity to meet, socialize and have fun with others who share similar interests, learn how to prepare delicious vegetarian cuisine with renowned cooking instructors, and eat great tasting, totally vegetarian food.

People for the Ethical Treatment of Animals (PETA)
http://envirolink.org/arrs/peta/index.html
PETA's website features Action Alerts which provide information on how you can help bring about a more compassionate world through simple, effective, direct actions. The Activist's Library gives visitors access to magazines, factsheets, videos, photos, and other related resources. The Compassionate Living page offers vegetarian

recipes, shopping guides, and more daily life ways to help the animals. PETA Kids is a new section of the website with all of the information kids, parents, and educators need to get more involved in animal rights.

Physicians Committee for Responsible Medicine (PCRM)
http://www.sai.com/pcrm/
PCRM is a non-profit organization comprised of doctors and laypersons working together for compassionate and effective medical practice, research and health promotion. This website offers News Releases and a guide to private health foundations. The guide identifies which foundations fund animal research, and those that do not. PCRM promotes preventive medicine through innovative programs such as The Gold Plan, a program for healthful eating for businesses, hospitals, and schools, and The New Four Food Groups is PCRM's innovative proposal for a federal nutrition policy that puts a new priority on health.

The Doctor is In...Charles Attwood, M.D., F.A.A.P.
http://www.vegsource.com/attwood/
Renowned pediatrician and author Dr. Charles Attwood is committed to helping you and your children make the transition to a healthy, low-fat, vegetarian diet. At this colorful and informative website you can get answers to health questions, read insightful articles on diet and nutrition, and review or post messages on a variety of health, diet, and fitness discussion boards.

The Jewish Vegan Lifestyle
http://www.goodnet.com/~tjvmab/
The purpose of The Jewish Vegan Lifestyle is to promote the practice of a vegan lifestyle within the Torah laws, both written and oral. At this website you will find Veggie-Rebbie frequently asked questions and answers, Jewish Vegan/ Vegetarian contacts, a worldwide events calendar, book reviews, kosher food alerts, a guide to Kosher Vegan and Vegetarian Restaurants, and personals listings for single Jewish Vegans and Vegetarians.

Vegan Action
http://www.vegan.org/
Vegan Action is a non-profit grassroots activist organization focused on promoting the vegan diet and lifestyle and inspiring more people to become actively involved in the vegan movement.

Vegetarian Pages
http://www.veg.org/veg/
Intended to be the definitive guide to what is available on the Internet for vegetarians, vegans and others.

Vegetarian Resource Group
http://www.vrg.org/
Here visitors can play a game and test their nutritional knowledge. You can sign up for VRG's free e-mail newsletter VRG-News and subscribe to the Vegetarian Journal online. Also check out VRG's catalogue featuring books about vegetarianism, magazines, t-shirts, and bumper stickers.

Vegetarian Society U.K.
http://www.veg.org/veg/Orgs/VegSocUK/
Established in 1847, The Vegetarian Society's aim is to increase the number of vegetarians in order to save animals, benefit human health and protect the environment and world food resources. The Society, a registered charity, is dedicated to fund-raising to drive its programs in campaigning, education, information and research. Their website is a resource for the new vegetarian, and provides information on health and nutrition, animals and the environment, a recipes index, and the youth pages, devoted specifically to young people interested in vegetarianism.

Vegetarian Union of North America (VUNA)
http://www.ivu.org/vuna/
This multi-lingual website is dedicated to promoting a strong, effective, cooperative vegetarian movement throughout North America. VUNA's aim is to supply vegetarian organizations and individuals with information

that will help them organize and maintain a strong vegetarian lifestyle.

Vegetarian Youth Network
http://www.geocities.com/RodeoDrive/1154/
The Vegetarian Youth Network is an informal, grassroots, non-professional organization run entirely by, and for, teenagers who support compassionate, healthy, globally-aware, vegetarian/vegan living. The Network is committed to providing support and encouragement to vegetarian youth through programs that emphasize communication (i.e. mail, phone, and e-mail).

Veggies Unite!
http://www.vegweb.com/
A wonderful resource for vegetarians featuring a chat room, weekly newsletter, a useful grocery list maker and weekly meal planner, book reviews, a recipe directory to over 2,000 vegan recipes, articles, and more.

VegSource
http://www.vegsource.com/
Your news, information and discussion site for all things related to vegetarianism, animals, the environment, and more.

World Guide to Vegetarianism
http://catless.ncl.ac.uk/veg/Guide/
A massive listing of vegetarian and vegetarian-friendly restaurants, stores, organizations, and services.

Glossary

Amaranth　　An ancient Aztec grain, ranging in color from purple to yellow. High in fiber, and rich in calcium, iron, and phosphorus, amaranth is also gluten-free.

Amazake　　A refreshing Japanese drink made from organic whole grain brown rice. Cultured rice (called koji) is added to the cooled whole grain allowing a natural sweetness to develop creating a flavorful nectar-like beverage.

Babaganoush　　Middle Eastern puree of eggplant, sesame seed paste, olive oil, lemon juice, and garlic which is served as a spread or dip.

Burrito　　From Mexican cookery, a folded and rolled flour tortilla stuffed with various savory fillings. Vegetarian burritos may be filled with shredded or chopped vegetables, cheese, or beans.

Basmati Rice　　An East Indian specialty of long grain rice which is aged for a year to enhance its flavor. It has a chewy texture and a nutty taste.

Calzone　　From Italy, a calzone is a large, stuffed turnover. Baked or fried, the fillings can be made from various vegetables or cheeses.

Chapati　　An unleavened round, flat bread from India, usually made from a simple mixture of whole-wheat flour and water.

Chicory　　A perennial plant often cultivated for its root, which when roasted and ground is used as a substitute or additive to coffee.

Chipotle Chile　Jalapeño chile with a sweet, smoky flavor.

Chorizo　　Used in both Mexican and Spanish cooking, chorizo is a highly seasoned, coarsely ground sausage flavored with garlic, chili powder and other spices. Before cooking chorizo, the casing is removed and the sausage is crumbled. Vegetarian chorizo may be added to a variety of dishes including soups, stews, and scrambled tofu.

Chutney　　A spicy condiment from India made with fruit, vinegar, sugar and spices. Chutney is the traditional accompaniment to curried dishes. It can range in spiciness from mild to hot.

....

Couscous   From the Middle East, couscous is a cooked, bulgur type grain made from granular semolina.   Often eaten as a side dish, salad, or sometimes sweetened for a dessert.

Enchilada   A Mexican dish made by rolling a softened corn tortilla around a vegetable filling.   Enchiladas are often topped with cheese.

Falafel   A Middle Eastern specialty, falafel are small, deep-fried patties or balls made of spiced, ground chickpeas. They are usually stuffed inside pita bread with shredded lettuce, tomatoes, and tahini sauce to create a tasty sandwich.

Gelatin   A tasteless and colorless thickening agent, derived from animal bones, cartilage, tendons, hooves and other tissue used to make fruity gel-like desserts. Vegetarian gelatin alternatives are readily available (see kosher gelatin below).

Hemp Seed   From the plant cannabis sativa, hemp seed is a highly nutritious source of protein and essential fatty acids which rivals the soybean for its nutritional value. Hemp seeds have a nutty taste and are used to make a variety of food products including hemp burgers.

Hummus   A thick Middle Eastern sauce made from mashed chickpeas, lemon juice, garlic, and olive oil. It's served as a sauce, or as a dip with pieces of pita bread.

Jalapeño Chili Smooth, dark green chile peppers with extremely hot seeds and stems.

Jerusalem Artichoke   Also called sunchoke, this vegetable is not really an artichoke, but a variety of sunflower having a lumpy, brown-skinned tuber which might resemble ginger root. The name comes from the Italian word for sunflower (girasole) and has nothing to do with Jerusalem, as one might think. The white fleshy part of this vegetable is sweet, crunchy, and nutty.   Jerusalem artichokes are a good source of iron. They can be eaten raw, boiled or steamed. A flour can be made from this vegetable which is used in foods such as non-dairy yogurt.

Kasha   From Eastern European cookery, kasha is a cooked dish prepared from hulled and crushed grain that is then roasted.   It can be made of millet or oats, but in America kasha is generally made from buckwheat groats. It is often eaten as a side dish or used as a filling for knishes.

Knish   A Jewish pastry consisting of a piece of dough wrapped around a filling of mashed potatoes, vegetables, kasha, or cheese. Knishes can be served as a side dish or appetizer. Dessert knishes can be made with a sweet, fruity filling.

Kosher Gelatin Plant-derived gelatins made from agar-agar, carageenan, (a dried seaweed product) or locust bean gum. Kosher Gelatins are available in plain or fruit flavors.

Masa   Masa is the traditional dough used to make corn tortillas and tamales. It is made with sun- or fire-dried corn kernels that have been cooked, soaked in limewater, and then ground into meal.

Millet   A small, round, golden grain that is prepared much like rice and is rich in protein. It is often eaten as a hot cereal or can be mixed with seasonings and served as a side dish.

Miso   A staple in Japanese cooking, miso is a thick, spreadable, salty paste made from cooked, aged soybeans, barley, or rice. It's used in flavoring soup bases, sauces, dips, salad dressings, and main dishes.

Mole   This rich, flavorful sauce is a Mexican specialty.   Made up of a smooth, cooked mixture of onions, garlic, several varieties of chiles, herbs, spices, and ground sesame or pumpkin seeds. Some variations of mole also contain a small amount of Mexican chocolate which contributes richness to the sauce without adding too much sweetness.

Naan   An East Indian, white-flour flattened, round bread that is lightly leavened. It is traditionally baked in a tandoor (brick and clay) oven.

Pâté   Vegetarian pâté is made from a finely ground or chunky mixture of vegetables, mushrooms, nuts, or seeds. A pâté can be satiny-smooth and spreadable, or like country pâté, coarsely textured. Pâtés are usually served as an appetizer along with crackers or small pieces of bread.

Posole   A thick, hearty soup from the Pacific coast of Mexico, usually eaten as a main course. Vegetarian posole is made from hominy, garlic, onions, dried chiles and cilantro.   Often served with radishes, onions, chopped lettuce, cheese, and cilantro which can be added to the soup to suit individual taste.

Ramen   A Japanese dish of noodles and vegetables in a delicately seasoned broth.

Ratatouille   From the French region of Provence, a dish that combines tomatoes, eggplant, onions, zucchini, bell peppers, garlic, and herbs simmered in olive oil. Ratatouille can be served hot or cold, and eaten as a side dish or as an appetizer with bread or crackers.

Samosa   From India, somosas are fried, triangular pastries stuffed with a savory vegetable mixture and often served as an appetizer with chutney.

Seitan   Also called wheat meat, seitan is a protein-rich food made from wheat gluten. It has a firm, chewy texture making it an ideal substitute for meat (especially chicken). Neutral in flavor, seitan easily picks up the flavors of the sauces, spices, and other foods with which it is cooked.

Shoyu   Japanese for soy sauce.

Soy Sauce   A staple in Asian cooking, soy sauce is a dark, salty sauce made by fermenting boiled soybeans and roasted wheat or barley. It is used to flavor soups, rice dishes, marinades, and vegetables, and as a table condiment as well.

Tahini   A thick, smooth paste made of ground sesame seeds from the Middle East.

Tamale   A Mexican dish made of various fillings coated with a masa dough and then wrapped in a softened corn husk. The tamale is steamed until the dough is cooked through and the corn husk is peeled back before the tamale is eaten. Tamales can be savory, (filled with a mixture of mashed vegetables), or sweet, (stuffed with fruit or other dessert filling).

Tamarind   The fruit of a tall shade tree native to Asia and northern Africa and widely grown in India. Large pods contain small seeds and a sour-sweet pulp that when dried, becomes extremely sour. Tamarind pulp concentrate is popular as a flavoring in East Indian cuisine and is used to season foods such as chutneys and curry dishes.

Tempeh   An Indonesian soy food made from cultured soybeans which are then pressed into bar form. Tempeh is high in protein and chewy in texture, making it a wonderful meat substitute.

Terrine   A pâté that has been cooked in a container called a terrine or any other similar type of mold.

Tofu   Popular throughout the Orient, tofu is a white curd made by washing, soaking, grinding, and boiling soybeans, adding coagulant, and then pressing the substance into a solid form. It's available in different textures such as soft, silken, hard, firm, and extra firm. When cooked with sauces and seasonings, tofu easily takes on their flavors.

Tortilla   The staple bread of Mexico, the tortilla is an unleavened, round, and flat bread resembling a very thin pancake. It can be made from corn flour (masa) or wheat flour, and is baked on a griddle. Tortillas are used for making burritos, enchiladas, tacos, and a variety of other dishes.

Triticale   An extremely nutritious hybrid of wheat and rye which has a nutty-sweet flavor.

TVP   Textured Vegetable Protein (or TVP) is concentrated soy protein. It can be used to extend or replace meat in chili, meatballs, casseroles, and an endless variety of dishes. It is the base for many of the ground meat substitutes available.

Vinaigrette   A tart sauce of oil, vinegar, and seasonings, usually used as a salad dressing.

Index of Suppliers

Companies which sell products through mail-order are highlighted in **bold print.**

Adambra Imports, Inc.
585 Meserole St.
Brooklyn, NY 11237
718-628-9700

Adeline's Gourmet Foods
5036 Venice Blvd.
Los Angeles, CA 90019
888-773-FOOD

Alcala Enterprises
12824 Hadley St. #106
Whittier, CA 90601
562-945-1683

Allied Old English, Inc.
100 Markley St.
Port Reading, NJ 07064
800-225-0122

AlpineAir Foods
13321 Grass Valley Ave.
Grass Valley, CA 95959
800-322-6325

Alpursa
PO Box 25846
Salt Lake City, UT 84125
801-965-8428

Amberwave Foods
201 Ann St.
Oakmont, PA 15139
800-875-3040

American Health Kennels
4351 NE 11th Ave.
Pompano Beach, FL 33064
800-940-DOGS

American Natural Snacks
PO Box 1067
St. Augustine, FL 32085
800-238-3947

Amy's Kitchen Inc.
PO Box 449
Petaluma, CA 94953
707-762-6194

Aspen Pet Products, Inc.
11701 E. 53rd Ave.
Denver, CO 80239
303-375-1001

Backpacker's Pantry
6350 Gunpark Dr.
Boulder, CO 80301
800-641-0500

Barbara's Bakery, Inc.
3900 Cypress Dr.
Petaluma, CA 94954
707-765-2273

Ben & Jerry's Homemade, Inc.
Rt. 100
Waterbury, VT 05676
802-651-9600

Bioforce of America Ltd.
21 West Mall
Plainview, NY 11803
800-645-9135

Blanchard & Blanchard Ltd.
PO Box 1080
Norwich, VT 05055
800-334-0268

Boca Burger Company
1660 NE 12th Terrace
Ft. Lauderdale, FL 33305
954-524-4171

Boss Bars
PO Box 517
Patagonia, AZ 85624   *For mail orders call Morrill's
520-394-2370*   New Directions: 800-368-5057

Bush Brothers & Company
PO Box 52330, Dept. C
Knoxville, TN 37950
615-623-2361

Cafix of North America, Inc.
E. 188 Midland Ave.
Paramus, NJ 07652
201-262-4830

California Natural Products
PO Box 1219
Lathrop, CA 95330
209-858-2525

Cascadian Farm
719 Metcalf St.
Sedro-Woolley, WA 98284
800-624-4123

Cedarlane Natural Foods, Inc.
1864 E. 22nd St.
Los Angeles, CA 90058
213-745-4255

Celentano
225 Bloomfield Ave.
Verona, NJ 07044
201-239-8444

Cemac Foods Corp.
1821 E. Sedgley Ave.
Philadelphia, PA 19124
800-724-0179

Cloud Nine Inc.
300 Observer Hwy., Third Fl.
Hoboken, NJ 07030
201-216-0382

Col. Sanchez Traditional Foods, Inc.
PO Box 5848
Santa Monica, CA 90409
310-313-6769

Community Products, Inc.
RD#2, Box 1950
Montpelier, VT 05602
800-927-2695

Coyote Cocina
1590 San Mateo Lane
Santa Fe, NM 87505
800-866-HOWL

D'Artagnan, Inc.
399-419 St. Paul Ave.
Jersey City, NJ 07306
800-327-8246

Dandy Doggie
15 Woodland Ave. - Suite E
San Rafael, CA 94901
888-236-4568

....

Della Terra, Inc.
5438 Rt. 14
Dundee, NY 14837
888-DT FOODS

Deep Foods, Inc.
1090 Springfield Rd.
Union, NJ 07083
800-468-6499

Del Sol Food Co., Inc.
PO Box 2243
Brenham, TX 77834
409-836-5978

Doca USA Inc.
PO Box 6327
Orange, CA 92613
888-PET-TREAT

Dolphin Natural Chocolates
PO Box 701
Mt. Shasta, CA 96067
800-2-DOLPHIN

Double Rainbow Gourmet Ice Creams, Inc.
275 South Van Ness Ave.
San Francisco, CA 94103
800-489-3580

Dr. McDougall's Right Foods
101 Utah Ave.
S. San Francisco, CA 94080
415-635-6000

Dreyer's Grand Ice Cream
5929 College Ave.
Oakland, CA 94618
800-888-3442

Earth/Sun Farm
PO Box 99
Dixon, NM 87527
505-579-4246

Eden Foods, Inc.
701 Tecumseh Rd.
Clinton, MI 49236
800-248-0320

Emes Kosher Foods
PO Box 833
Lombard, IL 60148
630-627-6204

Equinox International
Phone orders for Equi-Milk
Item #3115 Reference #1160959
800-519-7777

Essence of India
PO Box 24568
Minneapolis, MN 55424
612-935-5999

Eskimo Pie Corp.
901 Moorefield Park Dr.
Richmond, VA 23236
804-560-8400

Evolution Pet Foods
287 E. 6th. St. - Suite 270
St. Paul, MN 55101
612-228-0632

Fair Exchange, Inc.
PO Box 534
Dexter, MI 48130
313-426-0989

Fantastic Foods Inc.
1250 N. McDowell Blvd.
Petaluma, CA 94954
707-778-7801

Farmhouse Foods Company
1550 Atlantic St.
Union City, CA 94587
800-847-FARM

First Light Foods
60 E. Elm St.
Chicago, IL 60611
800-555-4332

Follow Your Heart
7848 Alabama Ave.
Canoga Park, CA 91304
818-347-9946

Food For Living
2226 4th St.
Eureka, CA 95501
707-441-1926

Food From The 'Hood c/o Crenshaw High School
5010 11th Ave.
Los Angeles, CA 90043
213-295-4842

Frankly Natural Bakers
7930 Arjons Dr., Suite A
San Diego, CA 92126
619-274-4000

Garden of Eatin' Inc.
5300 Santa Monica Blvd.
Los Angeles, CA 90029
213-462-5406

Geetha's Gourmet Products
1589 Imperial Ridge
Las Cruces, NM 88011
800-274-0475

Ghirardelli Chocolate Company
1111 139th Ave.
San Leandro, CA 94578
800-877-9338

Glacier Gourmet, Inc.
25437 Rye Canyon Rd.
Santa Clarita, CA 91355
800-257-4947

Goldwater's Foods of Arizona
PO Box 9846
Scottsdale, AZ 85252
800-488-4932

Gourmet Tamales
2588 El Camino Real D-228
Carlsbad, CA 92008
760-729-0387

Grainaissance, Inc.
1580 62nd St.
Emeryville, CA 94608
800-GRAIN-97

Green Options, Inc.
2262 Palou Ave.
San Francisco, CA 94124
888-473-3667

Greene's Farm
PO Box 16787
Denver, CO 80216
800-748-2972

Guiltless Gourmet, Inc.
3709 Promontory Point Dr. #131
Austin, TX 78744
512-443-4373

The Hain Food Group, Inc.
50 Charles Lindbergh Blvd.
Uniondale, NY 11553
800-434-HAIN

Harbingers of a New Age
717 E. Missoula Ave.
Troy, Montana 59935
800-884-6262

Hawaiian Fruit Specialties Ltd.
PO Box 637
Kalaheo, Kauai, HI 96741
808-828-1761

Health is Wealth Inc.
Sykes Lane
Williamstown, NJ 08094
609-728-1998

Health Valley Foods
16100 Foothill Blvd.
Irwindale, CA 91706
800-423-4846

Healthy Pet Products
PO Box 2075
Sebastopol, CA 95473
707-829-2250

Heaven Scent Natural Foods Co.
2516 California St.
Santa Monica, CA 90403
310-829-9050

....

HKS Marketing, Ltd.
420 Kent St.
Brooklyn, NY 11211
718-384-2400

Holy Chipotle
369 Montezuma #451
Santa Fe, NM 87501
800-992-HOLY

Hormel Foods Corporation
1 Hormel Place
Austin, MN 55912
800-523-4635

Hot Mama's Ravioli, Etc.
1485 Gericke Rd.
Petaluma, CA 94952
707-778-3441

Howler Products
2685 Elizabeth Court
Sebastopol, CA 95472
800-HOWLERS

Hunt-Wesson, Inc.
PO Box 4800
Fullerton, CA 92634
800-633-0112

Imagine Foods, Inc.
350 Cambridge Ave., Suite #350
Palo Alto, CA 94306
415-327-1444

Integrated Brands Inc.
4175 Veterans Hwy.
Ronkonkoma, NY 11779
800-423-2763

International ProSoya Corp.
312-19292 60th Ave.
Surrey, BC V3S 8E5 Canada
604-532-8030

J&J Snack Foods Corp.
5353 Downey Rd.
Vernon, CA 90058
213-851-0171

Jacqui's Gourmet Cookies, Etc.
664A Freeman Ln. - Suite 204
Grass Valley, CA 95949
800-310-0107

The Just Tomatoes Company
PO Box 807
Westley, CA 95387
800-537-1985

Kali's Sportnaturals, Inc.
1610 Fifth St.
Berkeley, CA 94710
800-884-KALI

Kraft General Foods, Inc.
250 North St., Box PC7
White Plains, NY 10625
800-432-6333

Knishworks
PO Box 454
Rosendale, NY 12472
914-658-9584

Knudsen & Sons, Inc.
PO Box 369
Chico, CA 95927
916-899-5010

Liberty Richter Inc.
400 Lyster Ave.
Saddle Brook, NJ 07663
201-843-8900

Lightlife Foods, Inc.
PO Box 870
Greenfield, MA 01302
800-274-6001

Little Bear Organic Foods
1065 E. Walnut St.
Carson, CA 90746
800-769-6455

Lucky Food Co.
1406 E. Stark St.
Portland, OR 97214
503-232-4873

Lumen Foods
409 Scott St.
Lake Charles, LA 70601
800-256-2253

Made In Nature
4340 Redwood Hwy., F236
San Rafael, CA 94903
800-90-ORGANIC

Maharishi Ayur-Ved Products International, Inc.
PO Box 49667
Colorado Springs, CO 80949
800-255-8332

Marscell The Organic Gourmet
PO Box 15214
San Luis Obispo, CA 93406
805-549-0920

Martin Brothers
PO Box 1686
Austin, TX 78767
512-478-4434

Mercantile Food Company
Carpenter Road, PO Box SS
Philmont, NY 12565
518-672-0190

Milagro Country Foods
1800 Central Ave. SE
Albuquerque, NM 87106
800-MILAGRO

Modern Products Inc.
PO Box 09398
Milwaukee, WI 53209
414-352-3333

Morinaga Nutritional Foods, Inc.
2050 W. 190th St., Suite 110
Torrance, CA 90504
800-NOW-TOFU

Mrs. Malibu Foods, Inc.
23852 PCH - Suite 372
Malibu, CA 90265
888-MRS. MALIBU

Mudpie Frozen Foods
2549 Lyndale Ave. South
Minneapolis, MN 55405
612-870-4888

Nana's Cookie Company
PO Box 188
Solana Beach, CA 92075
800-836-7534

Nasoya Foods, Inc.
1 New England Way
Ayer, MA 01432
800-229-TOFU

Natural Feast Corp.
435 Coggeshall St.
New Bedford, MA 02746
508-984-4230

Natural Life, Inc.
PO Box 20492
Floral Park, NY 11002
516-352-5257

Natural Life Pet Products, Inc.
PO Box 943
Frontenac, KS 66763
800-367-2391

Natural Ovens of Manitowoc Wisconsin
PO Box 730
Manitowoc, WI 54221
800-558-3535

Nature's Animals, Inc.
170 Bennett St.
Bridgeport, CT 06605
800-DOG-BONE

Nature's Hilights
PO Box 3526
Chico, CA 95927
800-313-6454

Nature's Recipe Pet Foods
341 Bonnie Circle
Corona, CA 91720
800-843-4008

Newman's Own
246 Post Rd. East
Westport, CT 06880
800-272-0257

Newman's Own Organics
PO Box 2098
Aptos, CA 95001
408-685-2866

Newmarket Foods, Inc.
2210 Pine View Way
Petaluma, CA 94954
707-778-3400

Nile Spice Foods
Box 20581
Seattle, WA 98102
800-265-6453

Nobull Foods
6987 N. Oracle Rd.
Tucson, AZ 85704
800-828-7648

Nordic Farmers
4848 S. Highland Dr. - Suite 211
Salt Lake City, UT 84117
801-272-9759

Northern Soy, Inc.
545 West Ave.
Rochester, NY 14611
716-235-8970

Orean's Express, Inc.
817 N. Lake Ave.
Pasadena, CA 91104
818-794-0861

P.J. Lisac & Associates, Inc.
9001 SE Lawnfield Rd.
Clackamas, OR 97015
503-652-1988

Pacific Foods of Oregon, Inc.
19480 SW 97th Ave.
Tualatin, OR 97062
503-692-9666

Papaya John's
PO Box 441
Paia, HI 96779
808-579-9608

PetGuard, Inc.
PO Box 728
Orange Park, FL 32067
800-874-3221 FL:800-331-7527

The Pillsbury Company
2866 Pillsbury Center
Minneapolis, MN 55402
800-998-9996 (For Green Giant)

Progresso Quality Foods Company
PO Box 555
Vineland, NJ 08360
800-200-9377

Purr-Fect Growlings
PO Box 90275
Los Angeles, CA 90009
213-751-3613

Quong Hop & Co.
161 Beacon St.
So. San Francisco, CA 94080
415-873-4444

....

R.F. Bakery International, Inc.
8101 Orion #6
Van Nuys, CA 91406
800-543-2555

The Rainforest Company
701 N. 15th St. - Suite 500
St. Louis, MO 63103
314-621-1330

RGE, Inc.
PO Box 23388
Santa Fe, NM 87502
800-838-0773

Ruthies Foods
PO Box 1029
Fallbrook, CA 92088
800-RUTHIES

Saguaro Food Products
860 E. 46th St.
Tucson, AZ 85713
520-884-8049

Sahara Natural Foods, Inc.
PO Box 11844
Berkeley, CA 94704
510-352-5111

Santa Barbara Creative Foods, Inc.
32 W. Anapamu St. #115
Santa Barbara, CA 93101
800-735-1565

Scenario, International Co.
PO Box 24177
Los Angeles, CA 90024
800-400-7772

Seenergy Foods, Inc.
121 Jevlan Dr., Woodbridge
Ontario L4L 8A8 Canada
905-850-2544

Sharon's Finest
Box 5020
Santa Rosa, CA 95402
800-656-9669

Simply Delicious, Inc.
8411 Hwy. NC 86
Cedar Grove, NC 27231
919-732-5294

Sovex Natural Foods, Inc.
PO Box 2178
Collegedale, TN 37315
800-227-2320 (call for free samples)

Soyco/Division of Galaxy Foods
2441 Viscount Flow
Orlando, FL 32809
800-441-9419

Spectrum Naturals, Inc.
133 Copeland St.
Petaluma, CA 94952
707-778-8900

The Spice Hunter
254 Granada Dr.
San Luis Obispo, CA 93401
805-544-4466

The Spice of Life Co.
15445 Ventura Blvd. - Suite 115
Sherman Oaks, CA 91403
800-256-2253

Springfield Creamery
29440 Airport Rd.
Eugene, OR 97402
541-689-2911

Stagg Foods Inc.
PO Box 39
Hillsboro, OR 97123
503-693-1999

Sun Foods Ltd.
115 McCormack St.
Toronto, Ontario, CA M6N 1X8
416-766-8214

Sundance Roasting Company, Inc.
PO Box 1886
Sandpoint, ID 83864
208-265-2445

Sunspire
2114 Adams Ave.
San Leandro, CA 94577
510-569-9731

The Tamarind Tree, Ltd.
1037 State St.
Perth Amboy, NJ 08861
800-HFC-TREE

Taj Gourmet Foods
190 Fountain St.
Framingham, MA 01702
508-875-6212

Teeccino Caffé, Inc.
1720 Las Canoas Rd.
Santa Barbara, CA 93105
800-498-3434

....

Timber Crest Farms
4791 Dry Creek Rd.
Healdsburg, CA 95448
707-433-8251

Today's Traditions
2560 Dominic Dr. #1
Chico, CA 95928
800-816-6873

Tofutti Brands, Inc.
50 Jackson Dr.
Cranford, NJ 07016
908-272-2400

Tradition Foods Inc.
8489 W. Third St. #1095
Los Angeles, CA 90048
213-651-1484

Tree of Life, Inc.
PO Box 410
St. Augustine, FL, 32085
904-824-4699

Tumaro's Homestyle Kitchens
5300 Santa Monica Blvd.
Los Angeles, CA 90029
213-464-6317

Turtle Island Foods
PO Box 176
Hood River, OR 97031
800-508-8100

Turtle Mountain, Inc.
PO Box 70
Junction City, OR 97448
541-998-6778

Uncle John's Foods
PO Box 489
Fairplay, CO 80440
800-530-8733

United Specialty Foods
PO Box 41279
Nashville, TN 37204
888-574-LIFE

Vegenarian
405 Allerton Ave.
So. San Francisco, CA 94080
888-328-4543

Vegetarian Health, Inc.
PO Box 525
Maywood, IL 60153
800-323-4092

Vermont Hemp Company
PO Box 5233
Burlington, VT 05402
802-878-9089

Vitasoy, Inc.
99 Park Lane
Brisbane, CA 94005
800-VITASOY

Westbrae Natural Foods
PO Box 48006
Gardena, CA 90248
800-SOY-MILK

White Wave, Inc.
6123 Arapahoe
Boulder, CO 80303
303-443-3470

Wholesome and Hearty Foods, Inc.
2422 SE Hawthorne Blvd.
Portland, OR 97214
800-636-0109

Wildwood Natural Foods
135 Bolinas Rd.
Fairfax, CA 94930
415-459-3919

Will-Pak Foods, Inc.
1448 240th St.
Harbor City, CA 90710
310-325-3504

Worthington Foods, Inc.
900 Proprietors Rd.
Worthington, OH 43085
800-243-1810

Wow-Bow Distributors
13B Lucon Dr.
Deer Park, NY 11729
800-326-0230

Wysong Medical Corp.
1880 N. Eastman
Midland, MI 48640
800-748-0188

The Yogi Tea Company
2545 Prairie Rd.
Eugene, OR 97402
800-YOGI-TEA

Yves Veggie Cuisine Inc.
1638 Derwent Way
Delta, BC, Canada V3M 6R9
604-525-1345

Food Index

....

....

145

Enjoy a **VITASOY.**
Banana Berry Whip

1/4 cup fresh or frozen raspberries
1/4 cup fresh or frozen strawberries
1 peeled banana
4-6 ice cubes
2 cups Vitasoy Vanilla Delite or
Light Vanilla Soy Drink

Directions:
Blend all ingredients
togetherin a blender until
thick and smooth.

50¢   **50¢**

The Canine Baker
GRANPAWS

Save 50¢
on the purchase of any 12 oz. natural dog treats

Doca USA, Inc. 1-888-PET-TREAT (738-8732)
24461 Ridge Route Drive, Suite 200, Laguna Hills, CA 92653

Redeemable at any professional pet retailer.
No Cash Value • Expires 12-31-99

50¢   **COUPON**   **50¢**

SOYCO *soyco* **FOODS.**

VEGGY SINGLES   *Rice*   **SOYMAGE**   **Wholesome Valley™**

5 77172 64135 0

GRAINAISSANCE

AMAZAKE
Smoothie Ideas

- Blend Vanilla Pecan Amazake with strawberries.
- Apricot Amazake blended with unsweetened pineapple makes a light, bright drink.
- Try Banana Amazake with any number of ingredients: dates, pineapple, coconut, cashews.

Retailer: Redeem directly. Grainaissance 1580 62nd Ave. Emeryville CA 94608

Ruthies

Vegan Organic Kosher Dishes

RETAILER: Worthington Foods will reimburse you for the face value of this coupon plus 8¢ handling, provided you and the consumer have complied with the terms of the offer. Void if copied, transferred, prohibited, taxed or restricted. Customer must pay any sales tax. Any other use constitutes fraud. Cash value 1/100¢. For redemption, mail to Worthington Foods, Inc., LMS Dept. 2690, P.O. Box 909, Tecate, CA 91980-0909. **LIMIT ONE COUPON PER PURCHASE.**

Worthington Foods

SPICE OF LIFE CO.
1.800.256.2253

**Do Not Double. Expires
12/31/99**

Retailer: Mori-Nu will reimburse you for the face value of this coupon plus 8¢ handling charge when properly redeemed. Void where prohibited, taxed or restricted. Cash value 1/100¢. Mail coupons to Mori-Nu, P.O. Box 6160, Torrance, CA 90504. Not valid with any other offer. Void when copied.

**Do Not Double. Expires
12/31/99**

Retailer: Mori-Nu will reimburse you for the face value of this coupon plus 8¢ handling charge when properly redeemed. Void where prohibited, taxed or restricted. Cash value 1/100¢. Mail coupons to Mori-Nu, P.O. Box 6160, Torrance, CA 90504. Not valid with any other offer. Void when copied.

Spoon it over brownies ...
Drizzle it over pound cake ...
Pour it over fresh fruit ...
Add to a vinaigrette salad dressing ...
adds bounce to your step , a smile to your
face and lifts your heart !

Consumer Coupon

Save 50¢

on the purchase of one (8.5 oz.) can of
Teeccino™ Caffeine-free Herbal Coffee

CONSUMER: Limit one coupon per purchase of specified product(s).
RETAILER: Teeccino Caffé will reimburse you the face value plus
8¢ handling only when redeemed by you from a consumer at the
time of purchase on product(s) indicated. Any other use constitutes
fraud. Invoices proving sufficient stock to cover coupon redeemed
must be shown upon request. Valid only in U.S.A. Void if copied or
restricted by law. Cash value 1/20¢. To redeem mail coupon to:
Teeccino Caffé, Inc., 1720 Las Canoas Rd., Santa Barbara, CA 93105.
No Expiration Date

Drip or brew just like coffee!

SAVE
50¢

MANUFACTURERS COUPON

SAVE
50¢

Jacqui's
GOURMET

LIMIT ONE COUPON PER ITEM PURCHASED

Committed To Good Taste, Good Health And Satisfaction
EGG FREE · WHEAT FREE · DAIRY FREE

MANUFACTURER'S COUPON   EXPIRES 01/31/00

SAVE 25¢

On Any Westbrae Natural Products

WESTBRAE NATURAL·   WESTSOY

BEARITOS

LITTLEBEAR
ORGANIC FOODS

One Coupon Per Purchase   **Do Not Double**

154 Coupons

To order a trial-size sampler including two flavors of Teeccino®

Mail $2 and a self-addressed, letter-size envelope to:

Teeccino Caffé
P.O. Box 42259
Santa Barbara, CA 93140

or call 1-800-498-3434

SAVE 50¢ — MANUFACTURERS COUPON — **SAVE 50¢**

Jacqui's GOURMET

LIMIT ONE COUPON PER ITEM PURCHASED

Committed To Good Taste, Good Health And Satisfaction

EGG FREE · WHEAT FREE · DAIRY FREE

25c On Any Westbrae Natural Products

You'll find our all natural products at natural and health food stores across the nation. Many supermarkets, too.

RETAILER: Westbrae Natural Foods will redeem this coupon for face value plus $ .08 handling. Coupon good only for product stated. Other use constitutes fraud. Void if copied. Cash value 1/100 cent. Mail to: Westbrae Natural Foods, P.O. Box 48006, Gardena, CA 90248.

BK

Save 25¢   On the purchase of any package of Instead of Yogurt.

Consumer: Coupon is good only for the purchase of one Instead of Yogurt package (any flavor). Any other use constitutes fraud. You must pay applicable sales tax. Limit one coupon per package purchased. Coupon is not transferable and may not be reproduced.
Retailer: McKee Foods Corporation will redeem this coupon for 25¢ plus 8¢ handling charge, provided you have accepted the coupon in compliance with all terms set forth herein. Any other use constitutes fraud. Adequate proof of purchase of products must be submitted upon request. No payment will be made for coupons which are mass cut, in mint condition or otherwise judged to be improperly submitted, and such coupons will be confiscated. Void if taxed, licensed, restricted, or prohibited. Cash value 1/20 of 1 cent. Send coupons to McKee Foods Corporation, PO Box 880591, El Paso, Texas 88588-0591, within 90 days of expiration to receive payment as set forth herein. Coupons accepted only from Retailers or clearinghouses authorized by McKee Foods Corporation.

200008

5 41648 00025   5 (8101)0 20000 1299

Thank you for choosing an American Health Kennels product.
Bark Bars,™ are made with love from the finest
all natural ingredients on earth.

Bark Bars™ contain no added salt, no added sugar,
no artificial colors, flavors or preservatives....

American Health Kennels, Inc.   4351 NE 11th Ave.
Pompano Beach, Florida 33064 • 954-781-0730

MANUFACTURER COUPON
DO NOT DOUBLE — NO EXPIRATION
LIMIT ONE COUPON PER PURCHASE

RETAILER: Wholesome & Hearty Foods, Inc. will reimburse you the face value price plus 8¢ handling only when redeemed by you from a consumer at the time of purchase on product(s) indicated. Any other use constitutes fraud. Proof of sufficient stock must be furnished upon request. Consumer must pay sales tax. Valid only in U.S.A. Void if copied, transferred, or restricted by law. Cash value 1/20¢. To redeem, mail coupon to: Wholesome & Hearty Foods, Inc., B&M Dept. 84059, P.O. Box 221, South Windsor, CT 06074

5 84059 11250 6   (8100)0 96036

.25¢ OFF   .25¢ OFF

ANY TURTLE ISLAND TEMPEH PRODUCT

Turtle Island Foods, Inc.
P.O. Box 176
Hood River, OR 97031

Expires: 12/31/99

Retailers: Turtle Island
will redeem face value
plus .08¢ shipping and
handling per coupon.

.25¢ OFF   .25¢ OFF

ORGANIC
BEANS & RICE
CHEESE STYLE

MANUFACTURER'S COUPON / NO EXPIRATION DATE

SAVE 25¢

WHEN YOU BUY CEDARLANE
LOW FAT BURRITO

TO THE CUSTOMER: THIS COUPON GOOD ONLY ON REQUIRED PURCHASE OF PRODUCT SPECIFIED. LIMITED TO ONE COUPON PER PURCHASE. COUPON CANNOT BE BOUGHT, SOLD OR EXCHANGED FOR CASH, COUPONS OR CERTIFICATES. ANY OTHER USE CONSTITUTES FRAUD. YOU MUST PAY ANY SALES TAX. TO THE RETAILER: Cedarlane will reimburse you for the face value of this coupon plus 8¢ for handling provided you have accepted this coupon in accordance with Cedarlane Redemption Policy herein by reference. Cash value 1/2¢.
Mail to: Cedarlane 1864 E. 22nd St., Los Angeles, CA 90058
COUPON MAY NOT BE DOUBLED

Low Fat
■
All
Natural

0 38794 34777 3

35¢ OFF   35¢ OFF

PURR-FECT GROWLINGS®

The Premier Pet Souvenir
Gift Company

GROWLINGS DOG BISCUIT TREATS

No Expiration Date

35¢ OFF   35¢ OFF

ORDER FORM

Mail orders to: Blue Coyote Press
P.O. Box 2101
Corrales, NM 87048

Please send the following number of books:
_____ books @ $12.95 ea. = _____

Sales Tax:
Please add 5.875% for books shipped to
New Mexico addresses.   _____

Shipping:
$4.00 for the first book and $2.00 for
each additional book.   _____

Total Amount Enclosed: _____

Payment by check or money order to Blue Coyote Press.

ORDER FORM

_____

_____

Mail orders to: Blue Coyote Press
P.O. Box 2101
Corrales, NM 87048

Please send the following number of books:
_____ books @ $12.95 ea. = _____

Sales Tax:
Please add 5.875% for books shipped to
New Mexico addresses.   _____

Shipping:
$4.00 for the first book and $2.00 for
each additional book.   _____

Total Amount Enclosed: _____

Payment by check or money order to Blue Coyote Press.